ASIA GREENE-RHODES

WORTHY

of

LOVE

HOW UNCONDITIONAL LOVE
IMPACTS OUR DAILY LIVES

Worthy of Love: How Unconditional Love Impacts Our Daily Lives
Asia Greene-Rhodes

Publishing and Design Services: MelindaMartin.me

For Kalen and Judah Rhodes
For my family and friends
Thank you for all your love and support.

CONTENTS

Envision this. A father and daughter hold hands and play in a giant field of flowers. Imagine, their contagious laughter among a background of beautiful birds tweeting their own melody. As the sun sets, the two head home with the girl on his shoulders. Now picture the father dropping his daughter off to school on her first day after packing her lunch. He's her partner for her first dance and the bond seems to be unbreakable.

In 2003, the bond I'm referring to felt like it would break. I was home playing with my toys when my mom called for me. I remember that day like it was yesterday: my hair was in two pigtails, and I was still in elementary school.

"Asia, come here," my mother said. "I need to talk to you."

In the bathroom, leaning against the bathroom sink, my mom stood. When I look at her, I notice how her dark brown straight hair is falling over her shoulders, her arms are crossed loosely over her chest and she's biting on her bottom lip. I'm fidgeting with my fingers and looking at the crumbs on her shirt and thinking about asking her to make me a snack, but I don't.

"Yes?" I raise my eyebrows. "Take a seat."

As she closes the bathroom door behind me, the blended scent of her melon cucumber lotion with her olive oil hair sheen gets trapped in the small room with us. I'm sitting on the closed toilet lid and even though my mom said a lot, there are only four words I remember…

"Herman is not your dad."

The bathroom walls felt like they were closing in on me, and the dull yellow light that illuminated the room seemed to go black for what seemed like an eternity. I felt lost.

I also felt confused and hurt. You would think I had a million questions on my mind and didn't even know where to start. But I knew exactly what I wanted an answer to.

"Why?"

"Wh —What do you mean?" She shifted her weight and rested her hands on her knees as she squatted in front of me.

"He is not your biological father because I already had you before I met him."

Before she could finish, tears were racing down my cheeks. My hands furiously swiped at my tears, but, with each one I wiped away, three more filled their place.

"Shhh, it's okay, Asia," My mom wrapped her arms around me. Her cheek was touching mine, and she was crying too. She held me a little longer before pulling away. "Now, don't get me wrong, by all means, Herman is still your dad, but your biological father would like to meet you today. It's okay to be afraid and confused; This is a lot. Herman will always be your dad."

I met my biological father that day, but we only exchanged two lines.

"Hi, my name is Asia" then he introduced himself and, after that, I never saw him again. Sometime later, I wrote a story about a dark shadowy figure and a light figure and how both were trying to pull me to their side.

I was confused and hurt in the story until I realized that the light figure had always been there and would always be there, while the shadowy figure was gone after a split second. This vision was my first encounter with unconditional love at a young age, though I don't think I would have identified it as such. Although the story was simple, I processed my experience and created my mental roadmap to help me find myself. This was the turning point in my life.

It wasn't until later in my life that I understood what unconditional love is and how it might look or how it might manifest itself in my life.

It has shown up in the work I do as a teacher; how I interact with my students and prepare them for life after my class and school, or in how I coach my athletes, or engage with my friends and family. No matter the relationship or the circumstance I may encounter, I find myself returning to the ultimate answer and solution, which is always to love unconditionally.

Love without limits means living a life of freedom. I desire this for myself and for those around me. You see, I have been writing since I was eight years old. My life experiences have always inspired me to write, usually poetry and short stories. All my adventures teach me something and help me realize some aspect of the truth about loving without limits or conditions. This not only makes me happy, but it inspires me to want to change the world.

When I wrote that first story at eight, my mom told me I needed to share this gift with the rest of the world. She explained how it is essential because you never know who else might be lost or going through something similar to what I had experienced. Someone could benefit from what I learn about the impact of unconditional love.

From that day forward, I started performing and sharing my spoken word in churches, at schools and universities, at community events, in front of community leaders, or the chief of police, or the mayor of Portland, at multiple Nike events, and finally at a TEDx talk in Portland.

As an advocate and fighter for change, when you are given a platform or opportunity to speak, you tend to use that platform to make a difference. I wrote a lot when I was eighteen and attending a majority-White college where I felt unwanted. In poetry class I was made to feel like my poetry style lacked the sophistication and form of traditional poetry or was too "street." I was often lost for words when I sat at my desk to write. Other times, when my pen hit paper, the words that came were those of a ferocious anger and hurt that could not be tamed. And when I presented those hot, but truthful words, I was turned away and advised to simmer down.

In those moments, I realized no one wants to listen to someone who is coming solely from a place of anger. If there is only anger, then there is no room for hope, and if there is no room for hope, then there is no room for change. It is only from a place of love that we can share our intense feelings, both positive and negative, and still get others to listen. It is the only way to inspire, and change hearts and minds. When I realized this, my destiny was already set toward discovering how unconditional love can affect all aspects of our daily lives. On

4

my nineteenth birthday I succeeded in writing and presenting a poem that was well received.

Every year I would experience some event or witness some scenario that would put me in the space of questioning what next? And always I had the choice to grow or fall back. Poetry became my release, but it also became my guide through difficult times. It wasn't until high school and part of college that I realized some of what I was writing about didn't apply to everyone or was just being ignored.

I decided to become a teacher because I wanted to teach writing, specifically poetry. I felt, and still feel, like everyone should have a roadmap for discovering their truths and releasing any baggage they might be holding on to.

I am a confident woman, emotionally, mentally, and spiritually who enjoys discovering the truths about life and because I understand the importance of loving myself unconditionally, which brings me to this book and to you. If you're reading this, you too are a seeker and discoverer of truth. You've found yourself in situations where you did not know what to do and just wanted to know you are not alone and where or when you should take your next step forward. Either way, in this crazy journey we call life, you have found yourself here in the pages of my book, seeking to confirm or discover new truths. What I will share with you in these pages will help you understand why you absolutely must love yourself unconditionally, and how unconditional love affects every facet of your life.

Imagine if you were to stop loving yourself. Of all the human beings in this world whose love do you think you might deserve most? Yours.

Love yourself so you can love others, and in turn, you can love the world. This is the journey I have embarked on, and I am fully aware that the learning will continue as I dive deeper. As a teacher, I have learned the art of forever being a student. As a mother, I've witnessed my own personal power at work. As a person who can see the beauty in full lips, big nostrils, basic brown eyes, and a crown of perfectly styled untamed fountains of locks, I also know what it costs to be different, to fit in, and to not. Life is my teacher, and I am a seeker of truth.

This book is divided into ten chapters with discussion questions at the end. Each chapter explains how unconditional love plays out in real life and where we can use it to create better outcomes.

I have learned many truths, such as the guilt that comes with motherhood, how parenting is rooted in unconditional love, and what it means to be married, happy, or in love. I share all of it in this book. I invite you to ask questions, form hypotheses, create theories, and discuss what you have discovered or relate to. Dive in with a friend and wrestle with the topics you feel comfortable with, as well as the issues that make your stomach churn and your head spin, and in turn, discover and form your own truth. Take a break when you need it. Analyze the poetry, engage with the prose and tackle the discussion questions. I also encourage you to get a journal and write your responses to the chapter questions for further reflection. Reflecting as you read can help you create a roadmap for your life. I hope my words help you feel inspired and empowered.

Thank you for choosing my book, and I hope you enjoy it!

CHAPTER ONE

UNCONDITIONAL LOVE

LOVE

You turn your nose up at what I wear.
To my experience you turn a blind eye.
And when my pain is exposed right in front of you,
your mind convinces your eyes that what just
  happened
could not possibly be real.
And then your lips part
and you show your teeth.
A smile right before
you poison me,
with those hollow words — you speak,

"I love you."

Please, stop!

Don't tell me you love me.
Before you let the words slip out of your mouth, void of
  all meaning,

trying to reassure me
that this simple phrase will cause comfort,
you need to understand this —
I do not believe you.

Because words without actions are empty.
They're just words.
So don't fill my ears with proverbs and verbs
you don't even believe.

Those utterances
make me cringe.
They're not a Band-Aid you can put on this
  gaping wound.
No! I actually hate you, but —
I love you.

Do I look like a fool?
Don't brush me to the side to end this conversation.
Stop saying it!
Show me!

To agree does not mean love.
To disagree does not equal hate.
You don't have to like who I affiliate with
to know I also deserve love.

So let go of your judgments and show me consistency.
Our political views don't need to align for us to stop

UNCONDITIONAL LOVE

tearing at each other's beliefs and
identity.

We don't need the same faith to
dance, sing and eat.
Our experiences may be different,
but they are all real.
So don't listen to say you listened.
Listen to begin to heal.

Love is not a check box you get to mark off
with penciled in words.

So no, I don't believe you when you say it.
Not until your love pours into my soul and
nourishes my very being.
Not until it wraps around me
when we agree, when we don't
and when you don't like me.
When it's not asked for and
I don't deserve it,
and still, it warms me.

When you don't understand my tribulations
Love is still required in all of my situations.

When you realize loving me means
loving yourself, even when you don't know how
to help.

WORTHY OF LOVE

When loving is what you breathe,
it goes further than turning the other cheek.

When you can love your enemies, truly.
That's when I will believe
you love me.

Unconditional Love

I have two last names: Mayo and Greene. My legal name, Mayo, was given to me by my biological father, and, Greene, the name everyone, including myself, believes is my real last name, is from the man who loved me since he came into mine and my mother's life when I was a baby. You see, my parents, my mother and stepfather met when I was a baby. My dad raised me as his own. In fact, my very first word was "Dada."

Because I was so young, my parents did not reveal to me that I had a different father until I was in fifth grade in which I was devastated at first. I quickly regained confidence, only to become insecure about my last name after entering high school.

The news about my real father left me devastated and insecure about my last name and what it meant.

In high school, a teacher read my name aloud as Asia Mayo instead of Asia Mayo-Greene. My palms started to sweat profusely as I squeezed them together in between my legs. The classroom seemed to shrink and grow dark as I tried to meet the eyes of my teacher who appeared to no longer be standing in front of the class but towering over my desk right in front of me as if she were actually six feet tall instead of five feet and five inches. Her eyes seemed to pierce through my flesh as my lungs struggled to get oxygen. I wanted to correct her. I needed to correct her, but my tongue refused to cooperate with my lips, so a slight head nod was all I could manage before she turned back to her attendance sheet.

"My name is Asia Greene," I whisper desperately to ears too far out of reach. I couldn't muster up the confidence to correct her during class, so I waited until the bell rang before I walked up to the teacher. As I approached her desk her once intense gaze seemed to have no effect as she glanced over at me "Hi, how can I help you?" She smiled.

"I know the attendance says my last name is Mayo, but I go by Greene." I said, shakingly. "Oh!" She quickly looked back at the computer where the attendance was then back at me again, "I will change that immediately, thank you for letting me know." I smiled and quickly exited the class. As soon as I took a step outside of the class I exhaled a sigh of relief, but my stomach was still uneasy.

The questions around my name would continue all the way through college. And not just in school but amongst my friends and in random conversations with teammates. There may be the slight head tilt or the rise of an eyebrow, followed by the gut-wrenching pause right before the first blow. One such conversation took place after church service when I was still in high school. It was late in the afternoon, and I was waiting for my parents to stop talking to everybody and their mom so that we could finally go home and eat. My stomach had felt like it was eating itself and the smell of hair grease mixed with sweet vanilla perfume was attacking my nostrils. I shifted my weight from my left leg to another and let out an irritated sigh after seeing my parents start a new conversation with another couple. A family friend who had previously seen my student ID card, which read "Asia Mayo-Greene" walked up.

"Your name is Asia Mayo?" He asked through squinted eyes as if they couldn't possibly understand the situation. But I know, they know because what else could explain it?

I have my mother's eyes, mouth, nose, head, curly hair, smile, eyebrows, ears, and kneecaps. I even make her same facial expressions. The only difference between us is her last name is Love, and mine is Mayo.

"So, is Herman Greene your dad?"

I want to scream, 'Yes! He's my dad! I have no other father!' But instead, I smile and offer a slight head tilt with a half shrug.

"Yeah, Mayo is my legal name. Herman is not my biological father." I nearly choke on the words as I finish them, all the while maintaining my fake smile.

Sometimes the conversation ends with a short, "Oh," and then I change the subject, or I leave and carry on with my day. But this time I was speaking with an inquisitive soul who did not want to stop with just one or two blows, but a complete knockout.

"Wait, how is that possible?"

He prods at the gaping wound. I'd like to roll my eyes and tell them my mom is like the virgin Mary, and basically, that's how I got here. Instead, I inhale deeply before explaining for the thousandth time in my life, "Yeah, it can be confusing," I give another fake smile, "My mom met my dad when I was still a baby and they got married when I was one, so I've only known him as dad."

"Oh yeah, he is definitely your dad" he nods continuously. I give another half-smile before making up an excuse to go to the bathroom. In the bathroom stall, I try to calm my pounding heart because I feel as though I had just fought a battle in which I had to defend my identity and my parents honor. When my breathing finally slows down, I straighten my back, lift my head, and walk back to my mom and dad who had just started another new conversation, but this time with the church mother. Another day, another internal battle of grasping at pieces of who I am.

However, it's not until high school when questions about my last name start to come up quite often when I find myself struggling to get back up after someone decides to play detective with apparent clues. I had just gone through another round of excruciating questions in class when my dad picked me up from school. I walk out the front doors and let the cool, crisp fall air hit my face. I close my eyes for a second and take another deep breath before I feel the bass of my dad's white suburban approaching a block away. It isn't until he turns on the street of my school and I can see our white suburban with twenty-two-inch rims blasting old school R&B that I feel my muscles relax a little more. The other students gawk at the sight of our car and loud music.

"Dang, who got the icy whip?" One of the upper class men says to his group of friends. "Yo, his bass slaps!" one of his friends replied. I look back to my dad parking in front of the school while he hangs his arm out the window waving to me with a huge grin on his face. "Come on baby girl, let's go!"

My chest puffs out and I hold my head slightly higher than usual as I skip down the stairs past the other students and to my dad's car with a huge grin on my face.

"Hey, Dad." I smile, my heart still pounding as we pull off. My dad is cruising, so we miss the first light and, like the yellow light, my excitement begins to slow down and my sense of pride begins to disappear.

"How was school, baby girl?" My dad asks, giving me a quick glance before looking back at the road. It's a red light and my confidence completely disappears. *Do I have the right to even have this kind of pride for having a cool dad when technically he is not my biological father? I have only known him all my life and have only met my biological father once. To me, he is my dad, but how does he feel about it?*

I smile because I know what I was thinking is ridiculous. Of course, he sees me as his daughter.

"It was fine." I try to shrug off the negative thoughts and breathe in the musky and warm smell of the suburban.

"Did you learn anything?" he continues, while driving with one hand on the steering wheel. His seat is reclined to the point that allows him to stretch his arm straight and rest on the steering wheel. His other hand plays with the stubble on his chin before resting on his stomach.

"I learned from my math teacher that if you have fractions and you want to divide it, don't even try it," I laugh, and then explain, "He taught us this by using one of Missy Elliot's songs, but he switched the lyrics so that it talked about math! It was so tight." I smiled. "Wow, that's tight. I wish I had a teacher who did stuff like that when I was in school. So did he just start rapping or . . ." He gestured with his hands encouraging me to fill in the blank.

"He told us we were going to learn about fractions and then he did the rap." I laughed and then we continued to have small talk. After another two minutes, we sat in the car together quietly just enjoying each other's presence and the humming of the car. I had thought I got rid of the looming thoughts that constantly caused me to doubt, but they quickly began to bubble over as we were only two blocks from the house.

When we finally pull into the driveway of our blue house, I grab my bag, jump out of the SUV and skip the stairs inside.

"Dad! Guess what?!" my little brother squeals as he and my two younger sisters rush to reveal some information they think is exciting. I smile when suddenly it dawns on me. They are his real kids. With that one thought I have instantly become an outsider to my own family. My lungs struggle to find oxygen, and my eyes start to itch, so I run to my room, close the door, and sink to the floor.

I am not his daughter. I sob, but I don't try to fight the tears back. I crawl into a ball on the floor, cover my mouth with my hands and cry a nasty cry. The one where snot pours out of your nose, and you scrunch up your face from crying so hard until you start hiccup which jolts your entire body. I cry until exhaustion takes over, and I fall asleep.

When I wake, my puffy eyes are sore, my throat is dry, and my lips are cracked. I sit up and crawl into my bed and struggle to stop the flood of thoughts filling my mind. *He can never love you like he loves his kids because you are not his daughter. You are different. As soon as you mess up, it's over. You are only here because you look exactly like your mom, so you blend in. Don't get too comfortable. Why would someone love another man's child?* I let out a ragged breath in the hopes of keeping down a sob, when I hear a knock on the door before it opens. I quickly sit up on the edge of my bed.

"Asia, your mom, said . . . you okay?" Herman asks as he walks to my bed and sits down next to me. I breathe for a second because I know there is no way I can hide how I feel from him and how he responds to what I am about to say next may confirm my worst fears. I close my eyes for a second and try to gather my thoughts before I ask the question, but instead, I blurt out, "Are you, my dad?"

"What? Of course I'm your dad."

"No, like," I pause because I feel the tears starting to build back up. "Do you see me as your real daughter or like different from Tashia and Taylor?" With those words, the tears are streaming down my cheeks, and no matter how much I swipe at them with the front and back of my hands, other tears fall in their place.

"Oh, Sweety." He pulled me into his arms. Immediately I felt warm and safe, but I knew this feeling was meant only for his actual kids. "From the moment I first saw you with your mother, I loved you. I have loved you since day one, and that will never change. Asia, you are my daughter, just like Tashia and Taylor. I've changed your diapers, watched you take your first steps, heard your first words, which was dad by the way, and your mom was not happy about that," He let out a small chuckle, "But I have been present in your life not because I had to, or because your mom forced me to, but because I wanted to, because I love you and see you as my flesh and blood."

"But what if I mess up, or get bad grades, or something?"

"Asia, you are my daughter, and there is nothing you can do to change that. Even if you hate me or decide you don't want me to be your father, I will always love you and do anything I can to support you and make you happy because I am your dad, and that's what dads do."

I breathe a sigh of relief and allow one side of my mouth to curl up into a grin.

"Okay," I whisper into his tear-stained sweater, trying not to get too excited from hearing what I hoped was always true.

When he releases me from his bear hug he smiles. "Do you feel better?"

"Yeah, I feel better." I wipe the remaining tears off my face, press my lips together and smile.

"Great, may I ask why you were feeling that way?"

I tell my dad about the conversations with people curious about my last name when I notice him tilting his head back and humming recognition of something as if he wants to explain.

"I wanted to change your last name, but your mom wanted to keep it to be respectful of your other family."

"Yeah, it doesn't bother me now that I know it won't change anything. At the end of the day, you are my dad, and my last name won't change that." I smile and nod my head.

"Exactly, I will always be your dad, and nothing in the whole wide world will change that." He wraps me in another embrace before he pulls back, "Now, I love you, but your mom wanted me to tell you, you need to get downstairs and clean that kitchen, so get to it." I laugh and roll my eyes and say okay as he leaves my room and heads downstairs. When I hear him finally reach the last step, I close my door, flop on my bed, pull my pillow to my face, and squeal and laugh into it until I have to refill my lungs with air. I sit up and smile to no one in particular, *I am Asia Greene*, I let out a chuckle before sprinting downstairs. It wouldn't be the first day, nor the last, that unconditional love would swoop in and soothe my heart. I knew I was adored and admired.

On another occasion, I am sitting in church while the preacher speaks about unconditional love from a Christian perspective. A selfless act and process of caring, adoring and admiring an individual because they are a child of God.

As I listen to the preacher speak about unconditional love, I contemplate on the selfless part of the definition. *How many of us can say we love selflessly? And what does loving selflessly mean?* I'm embarrassed to think of the many times I have been guilty of using phrases like, "I love you because you make ME happy,"

"I love you because you make ME feel beautiful," "I love you because you complete ME,"

"I love you make because you make ME feel worth it,"

"I love you because you give ME confidence."

I realize then phrases like these, mean I am saying that I do not love others for who they are, but for how they make me feel. I realize I have been loving because of what I receive in return. Whether what I receive manifests as a compliment, false confidence in myself, someone to always say yes, or provide financial support, or offer a helping hand, or even to return the love I might give, I am constantly receiving.

"Selfish!" The pastor exclaims. "We, as human beings, are selfish creatures."

I agree. But isn't it okay to want to be loved? I imagine having a relationship where both my partner and I want love, but neither of us is willing to give love unless it is conditional love. Then as if the pastor could hear my thoughts.

"Who would ever truly be loved or know how to love if we only knew the selfish love of humans? Good thing we have God as a teacher. He will never leave us nor forsake us. There are no conditions to God's love. It will never be; if you are perfect only then I will love you. God knows we will mess up and sin, which is why he sent his only begotten Son to die on the cross for us so that whosoever believeth in him shall not perish but have eternal life. In other words, God said I know you will probably fail, but I will make way for you anyway. I know you might hurt or betray me, but I will sacrifice for you anyway. I know you are imperfect, and there is nothing you can give me that will measure up, but I will love you anyway. That is unconditional love."

I sit in awe of the ideal and beauty of unconditional love. When you love selflessly, you love without expecting something in return. You love with every ounce of your being. However, to be Christ-like, I have to make sure I am loving without expecting something in return. As the preacher continues with the sermon, I reflect on what I am capable of and what I need to do.

As a believer, I am called to love my neighbors and those I don't even know. Love is a selfless action that I can't possibly achieve without God. And selfless action is part of romantic, familial, and platonic love. However, understanding that I must act selflessly does not mean I don't still struggle with the idea that I can't choose to love someone because of what they do for me or because of their actions, sinful or not. I'm not going to lie; it is difficult because sometimes I can be judgmental, especially if someone's actions impact me negatively. Or sometimes, I think I love someone, but my love is conditional because it's based on the positive impact that person has always made in my life. I decide I've been sharing only fake love when the preacher starts his third closing.

"We have to be honest with the world and ourselves. If we, as human beings, could love everyone and without struggle, then we would be perfect. However, that is not possible, so if anyone claims to, they are lying or they need a reality check." I feel relieved because hearing this somehow takes some pressure off of me, and I look around the church pews and wonder if anyone else feels the same way I do. The congregation nods and utters an "Amen Pastor" in unison. I take that as an affirmation that I'm probably on the right track.

The only being capable of perfect selfless love is God, and it is like Him I strive to be. In and through him, I am given an undying love that comforts me and expects nothing in return. There is nothing I can give God that will satisfy him. I toss my head back and chuckle a little because it is so mind-boggling to believe God loved me before I entered this world. A love like that is so pure and mighty it could only come from God. But I want to do my best to express this kind of love in my own life. I smile to myself, I have my call to action, but I realize I don't know where to begin. Who should I practice this unconditional love with first?

I scan the sanctuary and look at my family and friends when an unexpected question pops up into my mind, *Do I love myself unconditionally? I mean, is it even possible to love myself this way?* A flood of images flash through my mind, and my jaw drops. I realize that to love unconditionally, like God, I need to start with myself. How can I love someone else without condition if I don't even know how to love myself without condition? The pastor finally wraps up his fourth closing of the sermon and prays us out. I grab my bag and say goodbye to a few members before I head out the door. The fresh air hits me as I take my first step on my journey to discovering how to love unconditionally.

Discussion Questions

1. What part of love do you struggle with most? Why? What are your plans to improve it?

2. What kind of love do you find yourself needing help with, i.e., familial, marital, platonic, self, Godly?

3. Have you loved selflessly before? Do you still love selflessly? How was it? Will you continue? Why or why not?

4. Do you love your enemies selflessly? Do you love the people involved with or around you, selflessly in moments of frustration, anger, or despair? Why or why not?

5. How do you show yourself unconditional love? Even if you already do this, how do you plan to continue this? Be specific.

6. When you pray, do you pray for your selfish benefit, or do you pray because you want another person to heal?

CHAPTER TWO

THE KEY TO HAPPINESS

TRUE HAPPINESS

I've tried candies and chocolate,
running and walking,
therapy talking,
eye candy stalking,
how'd you get that mocking?

Just to fill this so-called thing they call void.
Tryna get someone to complete my sentences,
so, I can be hashtag goals
'cause I want to be that happy in a photo.

But you wanna know something sad?
No-one on earth can give you the love or happiness
   you deserve or desire.
But you wanna know something amazing?
No-one on earth can give you the love or happiness
   you deserve or desire.
So, no-one can take it either.

WORTHY OF LOVE

Because you can't take what you can't give,
and love and happiness within us is where it lives.

There is no-one who can complete me.
With just God I am already complete.
I am the whole banana split,
the cake, I get to eat.
I bring the heat to the beach
'cause baby I'm hot!
And if you're in my life
you're just the cherry on top.
I'm the whole meal, yes, all real.

So, let's not get it twisted,
you may be a dessert,
but just having dessert will make your stomach hurt.
So, I can't keep trying to fill this void with cookies
    and cakes
until I make sure
me, myself, and I
are the full and complete plate.

That's happiness,
and along those lines it's been viewed and
    misconstrued
as someone coming and giving us something
that we were never meant nor created to give,
so we confuse these substitutions as
solutions to our emptiness,

THE KEY TO HAPPINESS

but what they forgot to tell us was —
we weren't empty to begin with.

Happiness,
realizing you are already
enough.

Starting with myself

How did I get here? How did I become a victim to conditional love? When I stepped out of church, I was supposed to start this life-changing journey in discovering how to love unconditionally, but how can I move forward if I don't even know how I got here?

So here I am, sitting in my room trying to figure out where I went wrong. I'm lying on my back with my legs dangling off the bed watching Sunkiss Alba, a Dominican YouTuber, demonstrate her curly hair routine. I watch as she detangles her hair with coconut oil and then washes and styles it until her perfect silk black ringlets fall over her shoulders. The final result is gorgeous. She models her hair from different camera angles, and at the end of the video, her husband comes by, kisses her, and everyone types in comments about how beautiful she looked. Sunkiss Alba looks happy.

I look at my heat-damaged hair in the reflection of my phone and then run to the bathroom. I hop in the shower and wash my hair, making sure to take extra care of it just like I saw in the video so that my curls will end up looking just like hers. When I get out, I can see curls starting to form at the roots, but the ends are very straight. I head into my bedroom, throw some baggy clothes on, and rummage through my stuff to find some hair product, when I realize I don't even own one curly hair product. Then I grab my keys and head to Fred Meyers. A little frustrated, I went back to her YouTube description to see what hair products she used in the video so I can get the same ones.

I grab the products she listed in her description, pay at self-checkout and race home to try and recreate the curly hair routine in the video. Once inside, I find the small section meant for "multicultural" hair. After creating a mess of unique smelling products in the bathroom and probably putting way too much product in my hair, or not enough, I look at the lifeless curls staring back at me. *Wow, they look like limp noodles.* I say to my reflection in the mirror as I hold a twenty percent frizzy and eighty percent straight loc of hair. I breathe a deep sigh of disappointment.

Not willing to give up on my hair just yet, I read every blog on the internet and watch every YouTuber with naturally curly hair to educate myself. After several weeks I can confidently say I now know about every hair type, silicone, paraben, shea butter, Do-It- Yourself growth serum, and even how to correctly pronounce jojoba oil. I have tried finger detangling, finger coiling, two-strand twists, braid outs, and perm rods, but my hair still looks nothing like any of the videos I've watched. I want to look bomb with curly hair, so everyone will be like, *'Dang, she's beautiful, look at her hair.'* But somehow, I find myself, once again, disappointed while looking in the mirror at my mop of hair.

I pick up my phone and find the following YouTube video recommendation so I can dream about what my life would be like if only my hair looked as good as the person giving the tutorial. In this video, the beauty guru recommends a different product called Mixed Chicks. I get excited because this might be it! This might be my opportunity to be beautiful and happy. Now I know this might sound crazy, but I thank God I am a cheap person because I didn't realize I was in a trance. I looked up how much the product, Mixed Chicks cost so I could purchase it, and the price tag was almost twenty dollars. *'Girrrrrrl, they got me bent,'* I say to myself while looking at the product description.

In that moment of complete and utter cheapness, I realize that not only have I placed a condition for one reason I will love myself, which happens to be if I have healthy curly hair, but I have also fallen victim to the life of a consumer. Here I am attempting to buy a product and an idea that has convinced me I can have healthy hair without cutting off any heat damage or doing the work. What's worse is I have convinced myself I will be beautiful only after I have this naturally curly hair, which will only come from this product. I'm not going to lie, for a split second I was hopeful that somehow, someway science found a cure to give me happiness in the form of a hair product. I almost bought one more product to graduate from product junkie to product hoarder. And on the verge of a ravaging hunger for fulfillment that kept deepening with every product purchased while my hair did not miraculously turn into the chunky 3B curls in the tutorials, I finally woke up.

Reflecting on whether it is possible to set conditions for why I do and do not love myself, I realize I'm in danger of creating conditions that I ultimately project onto others. When I get caught up about something I don't have, I might start comparing myself to the SunKiss Albas of the world like I did with my heat damaged curly hair.

I was setting the wrong standards for why someone should love me and why I should be considered beautiful and happy.

I pulled out my laptop and, out of habit, went to a natural hair blog.

The first blog to pop up was about natural hair women who have a lot of products. *'Wow,'* I let out a chuckle. *'They got 'em too,'* I say, shaking my head. "They" as in the producers of the world who have tricked me into believing I can never be genuinely happy because how can I be content or happy with what I already have? Therefore, I must buy something else to acquire that happiness! I need something other than myself because there is something I lack, and every intelligent being on social media with their sponsored ads is there to tell me how I can be complete just by using my debit card.

The most famous "product" marketed to consumers for personal happiness is having a significant other. Being single has been linked to the absence of joy. We might not be sad, society says, but we are not happy if we are single. However, suppose I am not truly happy before I get into a relationship. Then the person I get into a relationship with can only provide me with a temporary sense of joy because the love I have for them can only be as deep as my love for myself.

It is just too much. I whisper to myself. I turn off the lights, put my phone on silent and close my eyes. Even if it is only for a second, I need to mute everything. After a minute goes by, the silence makes me feel uncomfortable, so I play with my hands. As I play with my hands, I notice I have calluses from lifting weights. *Yeah, I definitely don't have soft dainty hands to lovingly caress my future husband's face, but at least I have strong biceps, so I can lift him over the threshold!* I burst into laughter at my joke. When I finally calm down, I take in the silence.

Then I scramble to turn on the lights, and once again, stare into the mirror, and take in every aspect of myself. I grab a notebook, and for every part of me I identify as imperfect, I write down why it is perfect for me. After making a list, I still find some imperfections I don't seem to turn into a reason for why it makes me perfect. I stare at the list because I thought I was so close to understanding how to love myself unconditionally, but I am once again hitting a wall. On my list, I recognize I am imperfect, but I also point out the benefit of being different, even if I'm just making a joke. I look at the list one final time and count every imperfection and compare it to the parts of me I don't believe are fixable. My list is mostly imperfections that make me perfect minus two and not to brag, but that would be at least a B plus, which is above average! I smile. *I'm not perfect!* I scream, but I am perfect in my own eyes because I am perfect to God.

First off, way easier said than done. Secondly, although this is a good start, it is just the beginning of truly loving myself. When I unconditionally love myself as God loves me, I have to make sure to include everything: the physical and the mental, emotional and soul parts of me too.

As the oldest sibling, I have always been demanding and super critical of myself, and even before starting high school, I questioned whether I was worthy of love.

One school day, I'm sitting across from my parents at a picnic table in the park. A welcome brisk wind blows across my face and calms my nerves as I fiddle with the table's chipped green paint. We would normally drive straight home, but on this day, they picked me up early from school and I was desperately trying to remember if I'd recently done anything wrong.

After some small talk, my mom asks a question I didn't expect.

"Why don't you want to go over there anymore?" She leans her body towards me and tilts her head to the side as if she might already know what I might say.

My heart starts racing, and my eyes burn. What if they don't understand? Will they believe me? I'm scared.

"Asia?" my mom's face softens; I can tell she is on the verge of tears, "It's okay, you can tell us."

It's hard to breathe. I can't look at them, but I slowly tell them everything that happened. I don't realize I'm crying until I hear my mom sniffling. When I stop speaking, we listen to the wind and the leaves dance through the park. I felt disgusting. I feverishly pick at my fingers, waiting for a response. It came from my dad.

"The first thing you need to know is that what has happened is wrong. That shouldn't have happened to you, and we want you to know that we love you and are here to protect you." My dad pauses for a second to try and calm himself.

"I wish you could trust us" My mom interjects, "What your dad is saying is that we love you, and we always will. We want to protect you and your siblings, but why didn't you feel you could come to us?" I glance at my dad and then back at the ground.

"I don't care if he is my brother; at the end of the day, you are my daughter, and I am here to protect you. What he did was wrong, and I would never choose someone else over my kids."

I start crying because that's what I was afraid of. I thought he wouldn't understand because it was his brother. I tried to calm myself, but the tears were rushing down my face. I didn't tell anyone because I was scared. My mom and dad sit next to me. My dad to the left of me and my mom to the right. My dad seems to be there, but his eyes are clouded with a lot of emotions, so I can't tell what he is thinking. My mom does all the talking while my dad opens up to face me, watching my reaction, but I avoid eye contact.

"Your little sister said some of the same things, and at the end of the day, we want you both to know you both are our priority in life. We don't care who it is and where they come from. If they hurt you or try to hurt you, it is our job to handle that. I'm telling you this not because I think it is your fault at all but because I want you both to be able to open up to us and tell us when you feel uncomfortable, regardless of who it is, so that your father and I can intervene beforehand." My mom reaches her hand close to me on the picnic table but does not yet touch me as I have my hands tucked tightly in between my legs and my head is tilted back down so I can try to avoid any more eye contact with them. I wanted to feel relieved by what my mom's words, but I couldn't.

"My sister?" I whisper. "You said, my sister?" My eyes fill with tears again. *I had failed. I never went there alone. I am the older sister with two younger sisters, and not only was I afraid to say anything because of who he is, but I thought I was protecting my younger sisters as well. I thought I was the sacrifice. My chest tightened. Everything is wrong. Why was I molested? If I was not a sacrifice and my younger sister had to suffer as well, why did this have to happen to us? What did we do to deserve this? I cried harder. I failed, failed, I'm so stupid. I'm the worst big sister and daughter there is.* My parents embrace me. They tell me they will take care of everything and then we leave the park.

As we get into the van, I look at them. I'm glad to have my parents, but can't help the way I feel. I know what happened wasn't my fault, but I don't understand *why* it happened. I feel gross, as if I'd bathed in dumpster juice. Why would my parents love someone like me? Someone who has been tarnished? Why would my sister love me if I failed to be a big sister that could protect her?

When we arrive home the first thing I do is shower. I'm in my room getting ready for bed even though it's still early. I hear a knock on the door, and it's my little sister. We both stare at each other for a moment before she comes in and we both sit on my bed.

"Did Mom and Dad talk to you?" she asked. "Yeah, they did."

"What did you tell them?"

"Everything." My puffy eyes begin to squeeze more tears out.

"Me too," she starts to cry as I wrap my arms around her and squeeze her tight.

"I'm sorry, I didn't know it was happening to you too," I barely managed to get out the words between our sobs.

"It's okay, it's not your fault," she cries into my shoulder.

I'm supposed to protect you; how can you love me so easily? I think to myself. We talk some more before I grow tired and want to go to bed. She reluctantly agrees and goes to her room.

After I close the door, I lay down on my bed and scream into my pillow. *If my purpose is to protect her, then why? Why am I here to fail? Why do I exist? Why love someone like me?*

In that emotional state it was difficult to think straight, and to acknowledge I was far too young to take on such a responsibility, and that I deserved to be loved. It took months before I could love myself. Even after the therapy we went through and after my father's brother confessed and was put into prison, it took years for me to understand that if there was anyone's love I deserved the most in this world, it was mine.

In time I understood that to receive love and love others, I had to love myself. Trying to make someone else my purpose is only a form of loving conditionally. The problem is, loving someone conditionally can make you dependent on their actions, responses, and level of happiness. Giving conditional love means you both inevitably fail in the relationship, just as I failed with my sister. I was incapable of giving her the love she deserved because at the time, I didn't love myself. I had yet to forgive myself and therefore I wasn't ready.

It took years to realize I deserve unconditional love not just because I am Asia, but most importantly, because I am God's daughter and, as his creation and all of God's creations, I am perfect and wonderfully made. God did not mess up when he created us. I am worthy of love and dedicating my life to someone or attempting to love someone to bring me purpose or in an attempt to make me happy will not give me unconditional love but could, instead, make me hate myself. After learning how to love myself, which is a continuous journey, I know my true purpose. With the acceptance of God, I already have what it takes to be enough and to be happy. I don't need anything; although all other things are excellent and can make life enjoyable, life is already exciting and complete.

To accept God into our lives, we must repent of all our sins and truly believe Jesus Christ is our Lord and Savior. We are accepting all that God is: he is omniscient, he is love, grace, and all-knowing. This is just the starting point, of course. We must also read the bible and study to be more like him, living each day to be the best version of ourselves. While we attempt to be Christ-like, we must shed our unhealthy ways (things that provide fake happiness) so we can allow ourselves to experience all of God, and all that he is. Having a relationship with God will enable us to learn more about the world, but most importantly about ourselves. God gives us purpose, and purpose gives us happiness. A life of idleness, partying, or doing whatever without ambition is a life lived in darkness and a constant unfulfilling cycle. Even mythological gods who partied and drank and enjoyed idleness became bored and lost because they were not truly content with their lives.

One of the signs you are experiencing real happiness is feeling content with yourself and who you are as a child of God. Another sign is noticing you have the drive to continue to be the best you without the urge to escape the life you are building for yourself. You can identify the difference between healthy breaks from certain aspects of your life vs. running away from reality instead of facing it. True happiness comes from your relationship with God as you discover your purpose and the drive to work on yourself and healing.

Discussion Questions

1. What is your definition of happiness? How has your definition of happiness changed over time?

2. What obstacles hinder you from being happy? How do you address them?

3. When did you realize you are already enough, or is this still something you struggle with? If so, why?

4. Why do you think we struggle with loving ourselves unconditionally?

CHAPTER THREE

FINDING PURPOSE IN ADULTHOOD

ADULTING

We have bills and more bills,
postponed dreams and
harsh realities
reminding us that we can't have everything mom and
  dad have
because we're not at that point in life, so
what was once Frosted Flakes is now
Corn Flakes.
Lemonade is Kool-Aid
Bounty is Target brand.
Nike is Walmart and tissue is borrowed
from school, work, and the church.
No-one tells you adulting hurts...

It's hard out here.

Life is real when you can't go to an empty refrigerator
    and yell
"Mom, we need groceries!"
Nothing is the same
once you have claimed you're grown
and even if you don't
there comes a time where we are supposed to act
    our age.

Currently, no-one really knows the exact date,
we must change the way we dress,
the way we speak,
our thinking should reflect our years of experience and
the lessons we have learned from our mistakes.
We are a different species.
And then comes the word…

Maturity.

They say with age comes maturity.
Lies!
They say with age comes wisdom.
Lies!
They say with age comes . . .
all lies!
Who even started saying with age comes something?

Because we will always meet people who

might be the same age or older, but they act like
they are five, and we as adults will still have to deal
with them.
Of course, we have options.

Ignore them.
Pray they grow up soon,
and respond in a respectful, but direct way.

Choose the high road and remain cool
because we have rules
on what it means to be a mature adult.
Even though most of us break them,
it is hard to truly adult in a world
filled with people who are convinced
your age is what makes you grow.

Don't get me wrong
there are many highs from the adulting life,
like independence, self discovery,
chasing your passions and dreams,
Creating your lifestyle and a family.
Starting from the bottom and rising to the top,
forming new relationships, and bonds,
and eventually earning the big bucks.
But that still doesn't change the fact that
Adulting truly sucks!

Finding Purpose in Adulthood

In college while I try to understand purpose, I come to realize that I also do not understand what it means to be an adult. Does everyone have the same purpose and is it to become the best adult you can be?

In the days leading up to college, I felt ready. As someone who has always been independent, transition does not scare me. The days go by quickly before it's finally time to move into my dorm. My parents and siblings drive me and my belongings to the campus, where we unload the car and find my dorm. We decorate my side with purple, black, and zebra patterns. It doesn't take us long to put the room together, so we explore the campus and grab a bite to eat. When it's dark out, I feel a knot tightening in my stomach as my parents tell me it's about that time for them to go. I smile, hug them, and say goodbye, but once my siblings shut the second door after them on the way out, my stomach drops, and I start to cry. My parents rush back, and we all come in for a group hug. I'm scared after all, but I don't say it because I know my parents won't leave if I do. I need to begin this next chapter of my life on my own.

They finish comforting me and remind me they are just a phone call away. After one final hug they leave. I take a deep breath once the door closes. Just as I start to get ready for bed my roommate walks in. Her pale face is red, and it's obvious she's been crying. She is a small girl with long wavy brown hair that goes past her hips. Her eyes are dark brown, but from her crying they have a slight pink tint to them.

"Your parents just left?" I ask even though I know the answer.

"Yeah," she barely manages to get out the words before she starts crying again. I instinctively wrap my arms around her and, as if reopening a fresh wound, begin to sob myself. *It's our first night on campus, and here we are, two eighteen and nineteen-year-old girls who thought we were grown, crying because our parents said, 'see you later.'*

The next few days, I'm determined to start my college experience off right. I go to my classes and get homework done on time.

However, I quickly realize I have never had to study properly a day in my life. General chemistry feels like a karate chop to the throat and a punch to the gut. It is the one class I decide to look at the notes I took during class, but I probably could have scored the same low F by not even looking at my notes. I'm devastated and don't understand why I failed. I need to take studying seriously; I know it's what my parents would say if they were here.

Over the next few weeks, I call my mom for spaghetti recipes, and to ask countless questions. How to separate my laundry? What brand of dryer sheets to use? What's the best way to straighten my hair? I even asked how to spell my middle name! The first month of college, I realize just how dependent I am on my parents' knowledge, and it blows my mind.

When I turned a sweet sixteen, I thought I would be an adult by eighteen because I could legally vote, or buy a lottery ticket, or fulfill so many of the tasks I couldn't as a child. Oh, how wrong I was.

I remember going to sleep the night before my eighteenth birthday, excited for what was to come, only to wake up and realize no drastic change had occurred in the eight to ten hours I had slept. I still had the body of a skinny elementary boy. I was still broke, and my mom and dad expected my chores to be done before they got back from work.

Instead of dwelling on the lack of change, I decided to look forward to turning twenty-one. Surely an additional three years would change me from teenager to instant adult. But, sadly, after a sip of hard Freckled Lemonade from Red Robins, after turning twenty-one, I could tell being declared an adult by law or being given permission to do "adult things" by a certain age did not make me an adult. Why? Because I thought that if I did everything considered "adulting," then I would be perceived as an adult, but in reality, I was only playing pretend.

The difference between being an adult vs. appearing to be an adult is consistently and intentionally making decisions to create the life you want instead of entertaining friends, or strangers on social media's thoughts and opinions of us. I was more concerned about people seeing me as an adult and I wanted to be treated like one. I wanted to appear responsible, be ready to do adult things, and have my parents and other adults allow me to do more. So I could be taken seriously and contribute to certain conversations. I wanted to sit at the adult table.

However, being an adult is not that simple and requires much more than that. Being an adult is taking care of yourself, taking responsibility for your actions, and balancing when and where you can let the kid in you be free to do as it pleases.

Although the meaning of being an adult may differ for some people, the following responsibilities are the ones I have heard countless times for confirming someone is finally an adult:

Do you pay your bills?

Having bills to pay means you now have responsibilities you must take care of. In the world we live in today, you cannot live and keep assets without paying a fee. Having bills is one thing, but paying them shows you can maintain your life.

Do you have a place to live?

In the past, the norm was getting your own place right after college. But so much has changed. The expected years of college before graduation has increased from four to five. And now getting a job right after college is not always possible due to the state of the current economy. Finally, the need for financial literacy has been on the rise, especially in the Black community.

In my early twenties, after I graduated from college I moved back in with my parents. It was a blessing to get a job right away, but during my stay with my parents, I remember my dad asking me several questions that changed my perspective. He helped me understand how living with them, at least for a while, could have a positive impact on my future.

My dad and mom were sitting on the loveseat in our living room and I on the plush carpet leaning against the other light brown couch. "I can't wait to have my own place. I promise

I won't stay long. I'll just get enough money to get up on my feet and then I'll have my own place." I nodded confidently to my parents. My mom glanced at me with her eyebrows raised as if to say she wasn't buying what I was saying, before going back to playing candy crush on her phone. My dad, who was now looking at me from his computer, furrowed his brows in confusion as if he was really trying to understand what I had just said.

"Why do you need to move right away?" he tilted his head to the side.

"I want to have my own place like how you and mom did. Plus, I need to be an independent adult paying my own bills." I spoke confidently.

"Okay," He took in a deep breath, "I just don't see why you are in a rush to give your hard-earned money to some stranger when you could live with us and save up for a down payment on a home?"

"Yeah, I guess you're right." I looked down at the floor still trying to grasp if it would be smart for me to continue living with my parents or get my own place like they did when they were just entering their twenties. As if reading my mind, my mom spoke up.

"You know your father and I had to make decisions and live our lives a certain way because we had no choice. We had to find a place because we married young and we had you. On the other hand, you are neither married nor do you have any children. It's okay to want to do some of the things we did, but remember you are different and hopefully in a better place than us when we were your age, so there is no need to rush." She pressed her lips together in a fine line and then gave me a smile.

"You guys are right, I just want to be living life and be grown, but I see what you are saying." I nodded my head in agreeance.

Months later after my then-boyfriend asked me to marry him, a similar conversation was brought up. We were beginning our search for apartments to live in together after the wedding when my dad asked why we would lose money on an apartment when we could be putting that same money towards owning a home? Now, where we live in Portland, an apartment can go around the same price as a mortgage on a house, so financially for us, it would not make sense to get the apartment.

After our talk I realized my dad was right. I was more focused on the idea of being an adult and what I was taught by societal norms about adults and how they live, versus focusing on what made sense financially for me and my future family. If you have your own place, that's great. If you live with your parents, that's also great, as long as you are making the decision that best meets your future goals.

1. **Do you work? Or have some source of income to cover living expenses?**

   To take care of yourself, you will need a source of income. Without it, you will be dependent upon others to the point where you will constantly need to ask for permission to do stuff you should be able to do without question. Therefore, temporarily not having a job or not getting a job is different from just not having one or choosing not to have one because you prefer to live off of others.

2. **Do you have an adult mentality?**

Having the maturity of an adult is what seals the deal. An adult mentality will help you execute your dreams and stay focused on what is important and worth your time. When we think of maturity, we usually think of the ability to effectively deal with different social, mental, and physical tasks characteristic of one's age level. However, today, at twenty-seven years old I learned the psychological definition of maturity, which can only result from having the ability to manage emotional states.

Here's what I believe are good indicators someone has reached adult maturity:

- You prioritize your needs and responsibilities to guarantee success.

- You set healthy boundaries with family, friends, and strangers not only for your protection but for theirs as well.

- You own your actions and the impact they may have. You not only abstain from making excuses but strive to change negative behaviors and improve constantly.

- You are supportive. *All haters can leave the building!* Your focus is on how you can support others instead of trying to one-up them.

- You are open to feedback. Sometimes, we need to be told we have lettuce in our teeth. As an adult, we should be open to receiving feedback and the vulnerability that comes with it.

Being an adult because of your age is vastly different from being an adult based on your mentality. Your age doesn't make you an adult, but your mentality and actions do, and sadly, there is no law or handbook to tell you what to do as an adult and to keep you on track. Adulting is something you do. And it's more challenging to accomplish when we're not all blessed with positive role models or experiences.

Attempting to Adult Around Other So-Called Adults

The most difficult part about being an adult is trying to be an adult around other people who are supposed to be adults. Consider this scenario:

I'm running late for a meeting, and I need to grab some food from Fred Meyers. I grab something for lunch from the deli when I remember I forgot to put on deodorant. I rush to the toiletry section and pick up the cheapest deodorant I can find and then rush over to the self-checkout line because I don't want to wait for other customers talking with the cashiers, nor do I want to talk to them about how my day is going so far. As I rush to the self-check outline, I accidentally bump into another shopper. I quickly apologize, but they're annoyed and tell me to "watch where I'm going." Not looking for trouble and wanting to get to work quickly, I apologize again and get in line. The same person then gets in line behind me and, not convinced of my apology, begins to speak loudly.

"I wish people would watch where they are going or say excuse me."

"Some folks just have no common decency, like at least let me go in front of you in line after you knocked my stuff down."

I hear their remarks, and as the mature adult I am, I have some options for how to respond:

A. Ignore them, pay for my items, and leave the store.

B. Turn around and apologize again and tell them it wasn't my intention to knock their stuff down, and I am running late for a meeting.

C. Slap them and then cuss them out because I have already apologized one too many times, and clearly, they were not paying attention either because they would have been able to avoid me.

As I consider my options, I understand there are good reasons option C is best avoided. One being, it's against the law to physically assault someone. But options A and B are interesting and, if done right, might work.

While option A will likely make the other person look stupid, I also have to deal with the embarrassment of someone putting me on blast. And although I would like to think everyone will understand the situation and realize I'm not at fault, some people will side with the person causing the scene. As a member of an imperfect society, I have to accept this as a possible outcome.

In option B, by apologizing again, I can come across as a suck-up, which might not be a bad thing depending on the person causing the scene (because they might feel like they can take advantage of me now). Still, as I explain I'm running late, it might come off as passive-aggressive or like I am saying "Get over it!" which I am. This can either shut the other person up or add fuel to the fire.

The best thing to do when in a situation with an adult who might not have the same maturity level I do is ask myself, "Will what I decide to do make sense if my goal is to love others unconditionally?"

When I'm adulting, I have to monitor my actions and responses closely because when an appropriate and mature answer is given to someone who may be the age of an adult, but immature, I'm not likely to get the desired reaction. Now I mustn't get mature and respectful mixed up with what it means to be kind or nice. Not every response from a mature adult must be nice or kind, the truth can seem disrespectful at times, even when that's not the intention.

The most important realization is that it takes a lot of energy and patience to love others unconditionally, especially in moments when I do not want to love them at all.

Taking actions based upon unconditional love is beneficial to my mental and spiritual health in the long run. Conserving energy, avoiding unnecessary confrontation and acting with maturity saves me time, and energy and allows me to impact others positively. If we are called to do anything on this earth, it is to love each other unconditionally regardless of relationship, societal status, or appearance.

Adulting on Social Media

Social media exposes people, or should I say, people expose themselves on social media. Before social media it was easier to put up the façade of adult-like behavior, and only show those closest to us our true colors and sometimes immature ways. Many have been fooled into thinking that social media is a personal diary or a dumping ground for every single thought and idea. Others have found it humorous and entertaining to engage in trolling by posting outlandish or controversial statements in the hopes of starting an argument or getting a rise out of people. And sometimes to start a silly argument out of sheer boredom.

If you happen to be a troll, you now know what not to do. If you find yourself engaged by a troll, the adult thing to do is ignore them when they post, and know you have two options:

1. Comment respectfully

2. Put them in their place and make them feel stupid. Clearly this should not be the actual action, but every once in a while, it does pop when we have had enough.

Of course, your response may vary depending on the relationship you have, as well as, what they post, and the kind of person they might be. In my experience, if the person posting is someone you do not know personally or have an established virtual relationship with, the first option is ideal. If you're wondering why I didn't list a third and popular option, to block them, it's because sometimes blocking others because they have a different perspective is not ideal. Unless they're intentionally attempting to create negative and hurtful conflict, being open to different insights and perspectives can only expand your own insights and perspective.

Imagine if we only surrounded ourselves with people who think and behave exactly the way we do. That would lead to a very black and white perspective and view of the world. Our lives can only be enhanced when we engage with others who might see blue and red or yellow and green. I would avoid blocking someone simply because they disagree with you. Blocking others for sharing a different perspective than yours is not only immature but also limiting your personal growth.

Responding to comments you may disagree with on any online social platform takes time, patience, and effort. Many people gain a fake sense of confidence; in fact, we shouldn't call it confidence because it's not. They understand they can hide behind their keyboard and a screen in the comfort of their bedroom and sometimes in a different state or country, making them more likely to say something reckless because they believe there will be no repercussions. Due to this, even if you have a mature adult response, the person might say anything back just to be a troll, which means option 1 will most likely be the appropriate response for a lot of online stuff. So, the question is, when is it appropriate to comment back and what should our comment entail, and then when is it not okay to ignore a comment or post?

Adulting can be exhausting, and sometimes you will mess up and give in to the temptation of resorting to an unhelpful or immature response. If you do give in to temptation, recognize it, fix it, move on, and try not to make it a cycle. The more you practice, the more you'll grow into the adult you want to be.

Responsibilities as an Adult

It's important to understand what your role as an adult is and what it isn't. Below I've listed which are and which aren't the responsibilities of a mature adult:

Responsibilities:

1.	Your well-being	6.	Paying your bills
2.	Caring for your physical, mental, and spiritual health	7.	Pursuing and completing your education
3.	Following your dream(s)	8.	Managing your attitude and behavior
4.	Caring for your children	9.	Considering which best actions to take
5.	Excelling at your job or chosen career	10.	Choosing your words carefully

NOT Your Responsibilities (Other people's):

1.	well-being	6.	bills
2.	physical, mental, and spiritual health	7.	education
3.	hopes and dream(s)	8.	attitude and behavior
4.	children	9.	actions
5.	jobs	10.	words

What is listed under NOT your responsibilities may seem harsh, since sometimes it's difficult not to take on the responsibilities of those closest to us. Know you can still have a positive impact on others especially when you enable them to handle their own responsibilities. By all means, I am not saying teachers and doctors or parents should be unsupportive, only that there is a line that must be drawn if you're being held back from your own personal development.

A Specific Purpose

Knowing I have been called to love everyone unconditionally is great, but I can't help but ask, "What does this look like for me, especially if every human being in the world is called to do the same thing? "I was sitting in a leadership meeting when the speaker said, "Create a list. On this list, include all of the talents you have and everything you are interested in doing. Then narrow it down to a few options."

I quickly grabbed a pen and scribbled everything I was passionate about, every talent I believed I had and what I wanted to do with it. Then I began to cross items off my list.

When I was younger, I remembered being asked what I wanted to be when I grew up. I didn't know exactly what I wanted to do, but I knew I wanted to be involved with youth, writing, and sports. As I reviewed my list, I noticed not much had changed besides the fact that my purpose had become more specific. Once I had only one item on my list, I went home and prayed for guidance on my journey to practicing unconditional love and for how could I fulfill my purpose with the talents

God has given me. Before I could fully understand my purpose, I felt lost. I would ask questions such as, "Why do I exist?" or, "What is the purpose of living?" It wasn't until my sophomore year in college when I realized God places a purpose and calling over our lives, but often:

1. We choose to ignore our calling. This often comes from not believing our purpose will be lucrative, or offer a high social status, or that it is difficult to achieve.

2. We don't understand our calling. It doesn't align with our personal plans or our vision for the future. We don't see how we can fulfill it with our background, resources, or experiences, and it goes against what our family, parents, or community have told us.

3. We mistake temporary purpose for our life purpose. We choose to be a spouse as our purpose. But what is our purpose then if our spouse is not there, leaves, or sadly dies? We choose to be a parent as our purpose, but what happens when our kids grow up and are independent and no longer need us?

There is only one purpose over my entire life, and it is given to me by God. By trying to fill any emptiness or emotional urges I might have with temporary fixes, I lose sight of what my purpose is and what real happiness is, and I set myself up for disappointment. To fulfill my life's purpose, of course, I must pray, but also recognize the gifts and talents God has given me.

In Matthew chapter 25, there is a parable about a man who gives his servants talents (aka money).

> *For the kingdom of heaven is as a man traveling into a far country, who called his own servants and delivered unto them his goods. And unto one he gave five talents, to another two, and to another one; to every man according to his several abilities; and straightway took his journey. Then he that had received the five talents went and traded with the same, and made them other five talents. And likewise he that had received two, he also gained other two. But he that had received one went and dug in the earth, and hid his lord's money. After a long time, the lord of those servants cometh, and reckoneth with them. And so he that had received five talents came and brought other five talents, saying, Lord, thou deliveredst unto me five talents: behold, I have gained beside them five talents more. His lord said unto him, Well done, thou good and faithful servant: thou hast been faithful over a few things, I will make thee ruler over many things: enter thou into the joy of thy lord. He also that had received two talents came and said, Lord, thou deliveredst unto me two talents: behold, I have gained two other talents beside them. His lord said unto him, Well done, good and faithful servant; thou hast been faithful over a few things, I will make thee ruler*

over many things: enter thou into the joy of thy Lord. Then he which had received the one talent came and said, Lord, I knew thee that thou art an hard man, reaping where thou hast not sown, and gathering where thou hast not strawed: And I was afraid, and went and hid thy talent in the earth: lo, there thou hast that is thine. His lord answered and said unto him, Thou wicked and slothful servant, thou knewest that I reap where I sowed not, and gather where I have not strawed: Thou oughtest therefore to have put my money to the exchangers, and then at my coming I should have received mine own with usury. Take therefore the talent from him, and give it unto him which hath ten talents. For unto every one that hath shall be given, and he shall have abundance: but from him that hath not shall be taken away even that which he hath. And cast ye the unprofitable servant into outer darkness: there shall be weeping and gnashing of teeth.

The main message of this parable is that when God gives you talent (actual talent, not money), do not just thank him and do nothing with that talent, but invest in it and use it. It has been given to you for a reason and it will help you accomplish not only your purpose, but God's will, and it will help you be fruitful.

Discussion Questions

1. What are the five characteristics of a true adult?

2. At what age do you believe an individual should be considered an adult and should be adulting?

3. Do you believe you are a true adult? Why or why not?

4. What do you like about adulting, and what do you dislike or what is easy about adulting and what is difficult?

5. What tips would have been helpful for you when you were on your journey to becoming a true adult?

6. What talent(s) do you have? How do you see those working throughout your life and into your purpose? What do you feel called to do?

CHAPTER FOUR

MARRIAGE

THE TRUTH ABOUT MARRIAGE

Marriage is a God thing.
For it to persist through all negativity,
you, your spouse, and the holy divinity need to exist
  in unity.

Yes, we need advice,
but not hypocritical foolery.
We don't know it all so we can't afford to be conceited.
Only closed minds are blind to their demise,
tricked by their own disguise
by what is believed will create a happy life.

And then there's Communication…
Why is it so hard, yet so easy?
We know when eyebrows rise,
the nostrils flare and then
when we sit by them, they scoot away.
They are mad

but we ask anyway,
"Are you mad at me, Babe?"

Communication...
that's when it's easy.
You see,
no matter your similarities,
you are different.
Your culture, different.
Your experience, different.
So here is where we get into trouble.

We assume...
We assume we know what they are going to do.
We assume our knowledge, practice, and behaviors
are common in that of our spouse,
but we are wrong.

You see,
I like to wrap all my presents with wrapping paper.
I don't like using gift bags for Christmas.
I close the cabinets behind me because that's what
   you do.
I don't flush after I pee because we are not rich so if
   it's brown
flush it down and if it's yellow let it mellow.
I sleep with all my limbs on the bed so no monsters
   can get me.

MARRIAGE

I wear sweats to church and sit in the back and praise
   God happily.
For me, on time is fifteen minutes early.
I like it warm in my home,
but I can't afford the heat, so I turn it up to 70 degrees,
sit on the heater with a blanket just so it warms me
then quickly shut it off.

We have our ways,
and even though we both might change
we call each other's practices weird, or wrong.

Communication...
or should I say, language?
He likes touch,
but you prefer quality time.
And then people bring up this interesting word called
   compromise.
Well, how can you communicate with someone who
   speaks another language?
When you don't even understand your own and it
   changes?

See, it's not just communication we seek, but
   understanding.
But no one tells you there isn't an arrival point
because marriage doesn't have a destination.
It is a continuous journey of highs and lows.
The truth about marriage is nobody freaking knows.

There is no expert,
no map to tell you when you and your partner will
  struggle
and when you'll succeed.
Everything is played by ear.
So just make sure it's you, your spouse, and the holy
  divinity.

Marriage

I was shaking. I rubbed my hot and sweaty hands together as my legs bounced up and down so ferociously that the chair I am sitting in begins to vibrate. I thought I prepared well enough. *I did my hair, chose an okay first-date outfit: light high-waisted jeans, some yellow converse sneakers, and a matching unbuttoned green and yellow plaid shirt with a clean white tank top under-neath. But sitting alone at Starbucks, I can't help but lose some of my confidence as the time for him to arrive draws near. What if he doesn't show up? What if he sees me and doesn't like what he sees?*

I push the thoughts out of my mind and try to focus on the task at hand, pretending to do homework on my laptop while waiting for him. I don't want to be caught looking for someone just if they never show up, so I had to appear to be doing some-thing. Plus, I'm a college student, and I need to study anyway.

Today, I am going on a date. My first date with a guy I've been talking to for a little over a month. It seems like an eternity, but only five minutes pass when a busted white car pulls into the parking lot. It's him! I try not to watch him walk in, and I keep my head down as the Starbucks door opens. He walks up to me and smiles.

"Hey, Asia?" His voice is smooth and deep. I can't help but notice his muscular build under his gray sweater. He chose to keep it super casual, sweatpants paired with a sweater that hugged his biceps, which makes me question if I should have just worn sweats myself?

"Hey!" I smile.

He smiles back, revealing perfectly straight, white teeth.

"Okay, cool." There is an awkward pause before he asks, "Should we go?"

"Yes," I smile and nod as I quickly pack my laptop into my bag. I get up, and we leave Starbucks and head to the parking lot. As we get into his car, I get a whiff of his cologne or body wash, the scent is crisp but surprisingly refreshing. His car was a stick shift, which somehow impresses me as he starts to drive. We get comfortable with small talk on the drive to the restaurant. When we arrive, the small talk has upgraded from semi-strangers to comfortable friends just out to get a bite to eat. After the waiter sits us, we both scan the menu.

"Have you been here before?" He asks me as I look at the unfamiliar names on the menu.

"Uhh, no. I haven't even heard of this place until today." I avoid eye contact with him as I am a little nervous still.

"Really?" His eyes go wide in shock, "Oh, I thought you would have heard of it. It is kind of popular."

I look back down at the menu and then at him, trying to give a flirtatious smile I lean in and ask, "Do you know what's good here?" *Oh my gosh cringe I know, but a girl is trying here to flirt and clearly, I am not good at it.*

He smiles at me and leans forward as well, "Well, I heard this is good," the corner of his mouth curls up as he points at a sandwich on the menu. *Okay, so maybe I'm not that bad at flirting because it worked.*

"Well, I guess I will have that then." After the waiter comes and takes the menus with our orders, I lean back in my chair and clear my throat as I look around the restaurant before letting my eyes meet his. Our eyes meet and we both can't resist the urge to smile. I quickly look down at my lap while still smiling hard. "So umm, you come here often?" I tuck some hair behind my ear and sit up straight.

"No, not really. I mean my grandma has brought me here a few times, but that's pretty much it." He is leaning back in his chair feeling a little more confident now. We continue small talk even after our food comes out. He keeps me smiling throughout the meal. When we finish, we decide to go for a walk because we don't want the date to end, and we are both now confident enough to deepen our conversation. As we walk down the street, he makes sure I walk on the inside, so he can shelter me from the road traffic.

"I was really nervous when we met up at Starbucks." I confess

"Really?" He turned his head towards me, "I was pretty nervous too!"

We both laugh. "I was like, 'what he wore sweats to our first date!'" I tease him.

"What, wow that's crazy because you definitely told me on the phone that you weren't dressing up and that you were going to wear sweats, and here you are looking all cute with your jeans, flannel, and chucks."

I can't help but blush because he just called me cute to my face. "I know, but my roommates said they would literally kill me if I wore sweats on our first date, so I tried a little." We both laugh and continue to tease each other as we walk with no destination in mind. As we walked back to the car, we bump shoulders and hold hands off and on. I know it's a little cheesy but when we get to his car he opens and closes my door again and I can't help but enjoy his small acts of kindness and even protectiveness.

It's getting late, and we still don't want our date to end, so we head to his great grandma's house to watch a movie on the smallest TV screen known to man. He pops *I Robot* into the DVD player, and we sit close to each other while the movie plays. Neither of us is really into the film. I listen to him breathe and I feel entirely comfortable when he touches my hand and holds it. This feels like the best date of my life.

No long after having that thought, doubt sinks in, and I panic. *What if he doesn't feel the same? I shouldn't get my hopes up. Do I even like him?* I slowly slide my hand away from his as we continue to watch the rest of the movie. When he drives me back to Starbucks, where my car is parked, he says, "I guess this is it."

"I guess so," I smile back at him.

He takes a step toward me and wraps his arms around my waist. I circle his neck with my arms, stretching up a little to make sure my head reaches the crook of his neck. We stand in the parking lot for a few minutes, embracing and holding each other. It feels so natural and perfect to be in his arms. My heart skips a beat, and when we finally pull away, we say good night a final time. I get into my car and begin the drive back to my apartment when it hits me. *I like him.*

I'm flooded with excitement, giddiness, shock, and then fear. *What if I get hurt? Does he like me? What if he doesn't like me a lot? I can't afford to open up and be vulnerable because once I open up, that's when he holds power, the power to hurt me. So I try to convince myself I can't like him. If I open up to him, I risk getting hurt and being heartbroken, but at the same time, if I open up to him, I could also fall in love, get married, and be happy.* My heart and head are arguing when my phone vibrates, it's a text from him. My heart speeds up, and a huge grin takes over my face. *This is going to be scary, but I'm going to take the risk.*

A month flies by. We talk all night on the phone, FaceTime each other, and I eventually invite him over to my apartment. He's on his way to my place when I find myself in a similar state of panic like on our first date. My heart is racing, and I can't sit still. I keep re- tidying anything that looks out of place and everything that is in place too. Finally, there's a knock at my door and time seems to stop. He's standing at my doorway smiling, and I can't help but smile back at him.

"Come in," I lick my lips. If my heart could beat any faster, it does. "I have to go grab something real quick," I lie as I race up the stairs so I can pull myself together. I'm so giddy and happy that he's here looking all fine, and whatnot. I actually do a couple jumping jacks just to calm my nerves. When I finally come down the stairs, he's waiting for me in the living room, admiring the unfurnished space and blank walls because my roommates and I have not yet decorated it.

"Hey, nice place," he smiles while still looking around the room before letting his eyes fall on me.

"Thank you; you want to play a game?" "Sure, I'm down for anything,"

I suggest we play Heads Up, the Ellen DeGeneres game on my phone. As we play, we get into the game and show our competitive natures. Any awkward feelings before this have vanished and are now replaced with both of us laughing and flirting. Finally, after what seems like the one-millionth round, we decide to play Twenty-One Questions, which is interesting because it's not a game, but we do it anyway.

I decide to go first, "So what's your favorite color?" I smile knowing dang well I'm just trying to ease him in before I ask the bigger questions.

"It's blue what about you?"

"I don't have one, but if I had to decide I would choose blue as well." We ask a few more questions that are easy like that before I ask, "So what would be your ideal girl or relationship?"

"Woah, she pulled out the big guns," he laughs and licks his lips before turning the question back on me, "What is your ideal relationship or man."

"Oh no, no, no, I asked you first sir, nice try." I bit my lower lip and smile at him.

He groans before answering, "She has to love God, obviously. Ugh, this is hard. Can I do a different question?" he tries to persuade me.

"No sir! You don't know what you want from a relationship or what you want in a woman?"

"I mean I do, I just… fine whatever. I want her to be a family person 'cause I have a big family and I want a big family. Yeah, is that good enough?"

I laugh, "Wow, that is a short list."

"I mean there is more, but yeah I feel like that's good enough." He laughs, "What about you?"

"Same, honestly. He needs to have a relationship with God, be respectful, wants a family, blah, blah, blah. So, I'm guessing you want kids then. How many do you want?"

"Oh, that's easy, five."

"Five? I exclaim, "Oh my gosh that's a lot!" "Really?" he laughs with a big grin on his face, "Then how many kids do you want?" "I mean like four."

"Four! That's only one less than me." We both burst into laughter and continue taking turns asking each other questions.

As we ask each other questions, the warm feelings I've felt with him resurface. I find myself enjoying our time together and realize I'm falling hard for the guy sitting just a few inches away from me. What do you do when you are afraid of the unknown and of taking risks? You build a wall. The night went well, but I caught myself nitpicking in an attempt to build a wall so I can keep my heart safe. After our third month of talking and probably my gazillionth time saying to my family, *"I don't know if I like him"* my mom sits me down.

"Asia, this is a good guy, and you can either give him a chance or not, but just know that if you let him go because you're too scared, that is your fault."

I know she's right, and I know I have feelings for him. I'm just trying to deny my feelings because I fear falling too deep. I grab my phone and send him a text asking when he plans to contact my dad to let him know we are officially dating? He did it the very next day.

Who would have known that a year and some change later, we would get engaged, get married, buy a house, and a year or so after that getting pregnant?! Every day I am so grateful I took that risk and allowed myself to be vulnerable with my future husband. Demetrius Kalen Rhodes, I love you.

Now the work begins.

The funniest lines to ever exist must be, "And they lived happily ever after. The End." Why does every story of true love stop right when the story should be starting?

I think it's because the producers realize marriage is a lot more complex than that; you can't tell little kids after the beautiful wedding, "And then they lived happily ever after until about three months into their marriage when she started taking thirty-minute showers, and their water bill was too high, they got into an argument." Yeah, that wouldn't sell as well, nor is it as catchy. Although marriage is beautiful, we still need to know it is also hard work and loving unconditionally is not only the root of that hard work, but the reason for a marriage's success.

Now that we're married and we've had our honeymoon, the real work begins. Unlike any relationship I will ever have, this one has a contract where the other person, my husband, is promising to love me unconditionally. I am guaranteed love back, but not just any love, unconditional love. In my marriage, I've learned this can be nice, but it's also a pitfall because, at times, I might treat it as a condition and forget that no matter if he loves me back or loves me in the way I want to be loved I am still supposed to love him unconditionally. Of course, I'm talking about romantic love and not loving him because he is a child of God. I have been married almost four years, and I am still learning a lot about what it means to love my spouse unconditionally.

Minor situations will continue to arise and irritate us both. But now we finally see each other for who we truly are, human beings. Honestly, at the moment, I was pretty shocked to know my husband, the love of my life, would leave the toilet seat up so that I, his true love, could fall into the grotesque abyss of the toilet bowl. I know now it is normal to not like every aspect of my spouse, and he for sure has some things he doesn't like about me. Still, the key to loving each other unconditionally is staying vulnerable and continuing to communicate.

Vulnerability

Sometimes I'm annoyed and I say things I don't mean. "I'm not going to hold you."

"I'm not nice anymore."

"From now on, I'm going to speak my mind." "Being the bigger person is overrated," and on occasion, "Whatever, I'm done! I don't care anymore!"

What I mean when I say these things is, "That hurt, and I am not going to open myself back up to more hurt."

In the first year of our marriage, Kalen and I had our first big fight, and it was during this time I realized true vulnerability is scary. To be open with the love of my life sounds sweet and amazing, but to expose myself to the possibility of getting my feelings or ego hurt can be overwhelming.

After our argument, we sit down and remain quiet for a moment. We have never argued before. My heart is pounding out of my chest because I don't know what to do, so I ask a stupid and unnecessary question.

"Do you still love me?"

He smiles and rolls his eyes, "Come on, babe, are you serious?" He laughs a little harder this time, "Of course, I love you."

I smile and nod my head to the side, agreeing my question is stupid, "Yeah, I know."

"Do you still love me?" he asks, smiling. I laugh, "Of course I do!"

I don't know if it's because we wanted to confirm we were in this until 'death do us part,' or we were letting each other know that getting into an argument did not mean we stopped loving each other, but the confirmation felt good. Kalen pulls me into his arms, and I lay my head on his chest and smile. We aren't saying we love each other because it sounds cute, but because it is a reminder that every ounce of our being is committed to loving each other. We intentionally pray for each other, not just because he or I request it, but because we know we need it, and it's what we should do. We support each other's HEALTHY habits and dreams to the best of our ability. Whether it's physically, mentally, or spiritually, we're there for each other. We are listening to not just each other's stories of success and accomplishment but to our cries for help, attention, or compassion.

And because of our argument, I am reminded of two important lessons.

Lesson One: To have a relationship with my husband where he feels comfortable enough to share intimate moments of his life with me, I must be vulnerable and allow him to see some of those moments within my own life.

Lesson Two: Neither of us are paid professional therapists, doctors, financial advisors, and so on. When we love each other and have to deal with all that comes with loving each other and becoming vulnerable, we are defenseless to the whirlwind of disappointment, energy-zapping, time-consuming, mental, and spiritual burden that comes with attempting to love selflessly.

When we choose to love each other, we are also choosing to be vulnerable with each other, and that is when we open the door to the possibility of being hurt. But, when we choose to be vulnerable, we also open the door to truly making a difference in our spouse's life. Whether it is putting a smile on their face, helping them take one step closer to their dream, or one stepping out of misery. There is no better feeling than knowing our spouse is loved. Being vulnerable is a beautiful way of living and real, selfless love cannot be accomplished without it.

Communication

I am assertive, or so my husband and family tell me. When there is something on my mind or going on, I have no problem being straightforward with my husband or anyone else. However, my husband's communication style tends to be more passive. Continuing to look at our first year of marriage, most of the fights we had were the result of miscommunication or a lack of communication.

"I didn't even say anything bad," Kalen looked at me in confusion.

"It's not what you said, babe, but how you said it." I had just asked Kalen if he wanted to go with me to the store.

"If you want me to," he responded without even looking my way.

I rolled my eyes and placed my hands on my hips. "Whatever, you can just say you don't want to go with me."

"Huh? What are you talking about?" He's looking at me now, and by his facial expression, I can tell he really has no clue as to why I'm irritated, but he knows by my posture I am not happy.

"Babe, you might respond by saying, 'Yes, dear,' or 'whatever you like' with a sweet tone, but your face says you're not interested, which makes me think I'm forcing you to do this."

He nods his head, "My bad, I'm interested. I'm just saying I'm okay with whatever you decide because I have no preference."

I leave things there for now because I know I am no better. I definitely come across at times like I have a hot attitude just based upon my facial expression.

Learning each other's verbal and non-verbal cues has taken a lot of time, and I would say we are still learning.

Assumptions are based on a combination of a lack of knowledge and judgment. For example, in a marriage, we tend to make assumptions about our spouse or the situations in our relationship. The problem with this is we lack the knowledge we need to decide for two people and often our judgments are biased.

We all make assumptions we think are right when they really aren't. It's easy to identify wrong assumptions from right ones. A right assumption is when there is no doubt that what we are assuming can be wrong, for example, if a clown is wearing a clown suit, then we can assume that he is a clown. However, wrong assumptions can be like grandpa farts, silent but deadly. This is because it is not so obvious in the beginning that the assumption is wrong. For example, if you and your friend both have a clean house, you might assume you both know "how to clean" or that you clean the same way. Wrong! Although the end goal could be similar, we never know the journey it took for someone else to get there and that is where we tend to make wrong assumptions.

My husband and I quickly learned there are infinite ways to do almost every household chore and activity. There are also thousands of definitions for one word. For example, when I tell my husband, I want to clean the kitchen, that means I want all the dishes washed, dried, and put away, the garbage taken out and replaced with a new garbage bag, the counters, stove, fridge, dishwasher, inside the sink, and toaster oven all sanitized and wiped down, as well as the floor swept and mopped. The kitchen should also smell clean, so if it needs to be aired out, then do that as well. However, for my husband, cleaning up might just mean putting the dishes in the dishwasher and making sure none of the large items are on the countertops (but not necessarily wiped down).

Although this might seem trivial, in a marriage, little things can add up. wrong assumptions usually start off small, with you assuming you both have the same, exact definition of "clean," or how to fold laundry, or make the bed, or other shared and individual responsibilities. However, they lead to other, more complicated "wrong assumptions" like you assuming just because you're married your spouse completely understands you, or knows what you want, or can read your mind! That last phrase might seem outlandish, but how many times have you made a face, given the silent treatment, or made a comment and expected your spouse to react a certain way? How many times has their unfavorable response irritated you when you desired them to react a certain way but never voiced it? It seems like we would never ask them to read our minds, but we do it all the time.

They ask us if we're mad, and we say no. What we really want is for them to ask us a few times before we go into detail about why we're angry. So we sigh, grunt, stare at them, and even ask them what they're doing because we want them to drop what they're doing and give us attention. But after they say, "I'm watching TV, babe,"

We say, "Oh," and walk away instead of saying, "Can you give me some attention? Can you stop watching TV and cuddle me? Or can you just chill with me for a second?"

Communicating our desire and what is actually on our minds is the key to making sure we are not making assumptions, especially since none of us are capable of reading minds.

I have found the best time to communicate your desired actions or outcomes is before conflict can even begin. For example, if you know you want to have quiet time without phones or electronics on any given day, letting your spouse know before the day or planning for it the week before will help avoid your request being viewed as a command. You can also frame your desire as a question so it doesn't come off as nagging. For example, "Can you clean the kitchen today?" Sounds way better than, "Clean the kitchen today because I'm tired of doing it."

Expressing your desires in advance will also help you keep a cool head. Lastly, learn what your spouse likes. We are constantly learning how to love each other the best way possible, and we have to actively observe each other and ask questions to figure it out. It is okay to sit down and ask your spouse what they might want to do differently. What do they like or not like? Figuring out what is working and what is not working for you both is a good starting point before you add any additional requests for change.

Compromise

I hate the word compromise. It means to not get everything you completely wanted. I was pessimistic about attempting it at first, but then I realized compromise is a great way to advance a marriage instead of pursuing only individual gain. The fact is, there will be times when we want something and our spouse may want something else. When it happens, we still lose or give something up.

Compromise is especially helpful when both you and your spouse have a healthy immediate family. Let's just say holidays can be the most chaotic and exciting time of the year. Why? Because you both love your immediate family and want to spend time with them. Now that you're married, you're both forced to split your time with family. What once was a traditional Thanksgiving dinner at 7:00 pm becomes a new chaotic Thanksgiving feast beginning at 2:00 pm at your home, then continues on to 4:00 pm at your family's, and then 6:00 pm at your in-laws. The time with each family is cut short, and although you would like to stay longer at each gathering you can't because there is no way to justify spending more time at one family's home than the other. You must accept that your holidays will never look the same and the time spent with your immediate family has been altered forever. However, change is good. It may be challenging, but it is good. Although time spent with immediate family decreases, the time you spend with your newly formed family will increase, and this is good!

Compromise is complex and can feel like you are losing, but you are actually gaining. You are gaining a deeper understanding and connection with your spouse. Marriage is unlike any other relationship in your life because a contract binds you and God's expectation that you will love as God loves you, or at least attempt to. A God love is a selfless love and that means we must love our spouse and acknowledge that the world doesn't wholly revolve around us.

Sex

Sex is beautiful. Sex within marriage is fantastic. Do it, have it, love it, and do it some more. But sex can sometimes get complicated.

Some of the complications that might occur include:

- The Desired Amount: Sometimes one spouse has a higher sex drive than the other spouse, which is not a bad thing, but if there is no communication, guilt and resentment can grow.

- Previous Relationships: If a spouse or both spouses have been in a prior relationship in which they were sexually active, it could lead to insecurity or unhealthy comparisons.

- Trauma: If a spouse has experienced sexual abuse, and you are aware of this, you will likely need to be extra cautious and take it slow especially when your spouse is triggered.

- Communication: As I said before, you can't read your spouse's mind, and they cannot read yours, so you need to communicate what turns you on and what you like. There is nothing wrong with this, and it will only lead to more intimate moments for both of you.

- Different Cultural views on sex: Your role in sex and how you perceive it may be shaped by how you were raised, your cultural background, and sometimes the intensity of your religious practices (whatever those may be). For example, in American culture, it is common to see women as sexual pleasers. They are to remain pure or untainted by other men, and when they finally marry, the focus is more on the man's pleasure. To step outside of this is to be less than a woman and sometimes to be seen as second-hand goods, which can really mess with your mind. A healthier approach is to step back and question why these are societal norms, whether they make sense, and who they serve? Do they serve and benefit both partners in the marriage or only one? It's also important to understand and communicate your and your spouse's expectations.

What happens after you have addressed any or all of the complications listed above? You accept that there will be days when you do not want sex, and your spouse does, or you want sex, and they don't. It is normal to have different sexual drives. There is nothing wrong with you or your spouse. You are not a bad wife or husband for wanting to make love more or less, depending on the day, week or month.

It's also important to realize that marriage is not a sprint, but a marathon and sex can get better as long as you are in it for the long run with your partner. Do not give up because it does get better; in fact, it gets really amazing!!! Research, experiment, fall in love with your body and what you like and what your partner likes. Don't compare your sexual relationship with that of others because everyone's sex life will look different. If you are going to bring someone into something as personal as your sex life, then bring a professional (sex therapist) and not a family member or friend.

Sex is a love language. Like any language, we are not born knowing how to speak it, which means we need to learn and practice as much as possible. Practice will help you and your spouse gain confidence and communication will always be important. If you're nervous about having a conversation, remember to breathe and know you are not asking for the impossible, only to deepen the connection with your spouse and to learn more what they like and don't like. It will also give you an opportunity to share your likes and dislikes.

Aside from communication, you need to have patience. Don't give up, try new things and continue to practice. There is no ticking bomb about to explode if you and your spouse don't get it right within the first night, week, month, or even year(s)! Don't forget you both signed up for forever, so you have time!

Boundaries, Rules, and Guidelines

It may seem odd but even in marriage, there still needs to be some clear boundaries you and your spouse agree to. They may be simple, but you still must not only set them up, but discuss them so all expectations are clear. For example:

Guests

Who can come over, and what are appropriate times when they can come over? Think about the people you would assume don't need to ask and can just pop up. Now consider if that would be okay with your spouse? Just because they are your mom or best friend it does not mean your spouse will be okay with it.

Finances

Money is the root of all evil, but it doesn't have to be. Marriages end for financial reasons when there are no clear expectations for how money should be managed. As you begin to share time, possessions, and space, it is only natural that money is going to come into play. It is important to understand your own expectations for what your finances should look like within your marriage.

Some important questions to consider:

- What are your financial goals?

- Do you plan on saving? How much do you want to save per month?

- How are you handling bills? Do you want to split them, or should one person pay all the bills?

- How do you want the bank account to look? Do you want both of you to have access to the money with one pot or separate pots you both can transfer from? Or absolutely no access and my money is mine, and your money is yours?

Check with yourself as well because sometimes we think we have a "my money is yours, and your money is mine" mindset when what we really have is a "my money is mine, and your money is mine as well" mindset. You need to share how you feel with your spouse to see if you're both on the same page, and if you aren't, then you need to figure out a way to get on the same page.

Disagreements

How do you deal with disagreements? Do you want to talk them out or do you need time to think? How does your spouse feel about this? Do you remain calm, or do you get passionate and loud during a disagreement?

Sharing

Who are you okay with knowing your marriage's personal affairs? Is your spouse okay with this? What do you think you two should share? What should always be kept between you two? Your spouse may be an open book, while you may be private. Perhaps it's the other way around, but you two are better off discussing this.

House rules/Roles and expectations

Do you want a clean house? Who does the cleaning and cooking? Will this be split? If either of you doesn't take care of it, will that household responsibility always fall on one person's shoulders? For you or your spouse, this may not be an issue. However, if one of you is not okay with doing most of the cooking and cleaning, but always does, it may cause future problems. Is there a curfew? Is a call or text needed when you need to stay out late? Do you need to check-in, even if you're with family members? It's better not to assume anything. It may seem like common sense to you or to them, and perhaps, it's something trivial. Yet, the little things add up, and it's better to know what's important and where both of you stand. Again, what might seem like common sense could be new to some. Do you like shoes in the house or not? Do you both get a say in decorating the home or not?

Screen time

How much screen time are you okay with? When do you want to be off the screen and face to face? During meals? Before bed? Do you want combined screen time where you and your spouse have a show together or play games together?

Dates/Sex

What do you want? How do you want it, when do you want it, and how often do you want it?

Children

Because there is a chapter on parenting, I won't go into too much detail here, so, for now, consider having a conversation about family planning. Do you want kids, and does your spouse want kids? How many do you both want?

Counseling

Honestly, everyone should be in counseling, and that includes individual, premarital, and marital counseling. It doesn't mean something is wrong with you or your marriage, it is simply a way to teach you and your spouse how to navigate through some of the areas mentioned above. It can also help you process your own thoughts so you can truly understand how to love the way you want to love. Counseling is often seen as a responsive strategy in the hopes of saving a marriage. However, it's best used as a preventative strategy in order to grow and deepen a marriage so you don't have to get to the responsive stage.

Also, each type of counseling addresses something different. Individual counseling focuses on you and your experience, while premarital counseling prepares you both for marriage before you say I do. You work out many of the scenarios mentioned in this chapter and learn how you and your partner think as individuals, which may sometimes surprise you. Marital counseling is for the challenges as they come while you are in them and working through them. Each form of counseling serves its own purpose and is worth looking into. Counseling can help you work through past problems you may not realize are still negatively affecting you and your marriage now.

Also, consulting with a professional who won't have a biased perspective will be more helpful than sharing your frustrations with a friend or family member. Bringing others who are not emotionally equipped to advise you on your marriage troubles can lead to negative consequences with your spouse.

Sometimes sharing your frustrations with a friend or loved one can alter their perception of your spouse which could lead to judgement and other challenges. The final risk is receiving biased feedback which ultimately just won't work.

If you decide to get counseling, I would highly recommend premarital counseling for sure, and then you and your spouse can decide if you want to continue marital counseling. I would first research counselors with similar backgrounds as yours. In other words, my husband and I are both Christians, and so it would be beneficial for us to have a counselor who is also a Christian. Having this in common makes it easier for the counseling you receive to align with your personal views and objectives as they pertain to God's will.

When we went to marriage counseling, another factor that helped was having premarital counselors who looked like us. Having a Black counselor was a huge benefit because they had a similar cultural experience and could easily relate to the community we belong to. It also made it easier to open up about our thoughts and issues we needed to address. When searching for a counselor, you can ask friends and loved ones for a recommendation, just sure to do your research.

Lastly, while you can go to counseling online now, I would strongly recommend going in person. You need to be able to remove yourself from home and be in a neutral space. There is also something wholesome about the car ride to and from the session together. There have been times when on the car ride there or after the session Kalen and I really learned a lot about each other and the way we think. We also created our own check-ins for before and after. Some of the questions we asked are listed below but feel free to use them as a starting point for creating your own list.

Questions for BEFORE the counseling session

- Are you excited, nervous, or both for this counseling session? Why?

- Is there anything you are looking forward to? What and why?

Questions for AFTER the counseling session

- How do you think it went?

- What was your favorite part of the session?

- What did you think when they said _____?

- Did you feel uncomfortable at any time, and if so, when?

These questions allowed us to understand each other better but also provided the space and opportunity to continue having healthy conversations even without the presence of a professional in the room. This not only boosted our confidence in ourselves and each other but set the bar high for the way we should communicate and check in on each other on a day-to-day basis. These check-ins do not take the place of counseling. But they definitely enhance your relationship because, as a married couple, you should learn how to communicate with each other without professional guidance. While having a healthy marriage takes work, a marriage rooted in unconditional love will ultimately lead to personal growth and the marital relationship you always dreamed of having. Despite awkward moments and the occasional struggle with communication continue to love each other and give your best.

Discussion Questions

1. What are some areas of your marriage where you need to set clear expectations?

2. What are some areas where you realized you might not have a healthy example, or you just don't know what some healthy expectations might look like? Have you talked about that with your spouse?

3. What do you think about marriage counseling? Why would or wouldn't you be open to it?

4. What do you fear or what makes you the most nervous when you think about marriage? Why?

5. Do you have a healthy example of a married couple you and your spouse look up to? Why do you look up to them? Obviously, there is no perfect couple. Still, there can be couples who have relationships with aspects we admire and strive to have in our relationships, like trust, communication, and so on. Just remember that it might look different in your relationship, and refrain from putting anyone on a pedestal.

6. How do you push yourself to be vulnerable when you struggle to do so?

CHAPTER FIVE

PARENTING

MOTHERHOOD

It's your Sweet Hawaiian roll legs,
and your sausage toes,
the chunk
of your double chin,
has me feelin' blessed.
Or is this bliss?
Your arms relax
and I cannot miss
those eyes roll back
when you get that milk as I
comb through your hair
made of silk.

I say you're the future,
the best there is.
I just know there's no other baby that's cuter than this.
They don't exist
and no-one can persuade me

because your God-sent,
my little heaven baby.
And some might disagree,
but they're crazy.

Cause I can watch you sleep all day,
until I want you awake.
Just don't feed every second
for goodness' sake.

I hate to hear you cry,
even though that's what you do.
I'll pick you up, feed you and clean your poop.
And if you still cry, I'll cry too.
But I guess that's a mama's truth.
It goes to say I will always
love you.

Motherhood

Motherhood is a blessing. I've been a mom for over a year now, and I would say it's going well, or at least as well as it can go. I wake up several times a night to comfort feed my son. I am a walking food factory, who pays his bills, wipes his butt, bathes him, clothes him, and loves him with all my heart. At least loving a tiny person unconditionally is easy because I don't expect anything in return. And I can't help but love him after the incredible journey I experienced before becoming his mom.

Finding Out You're Pregnant

Finding out you're going to be a parent is like riding a roller coaster. It begins with a rush of excitement. Then the ups—moments of excitement—followed by free-falling drops—being consumed by fear and doubt begin.

"What will the baby look like?"

"What will we name it?"

"If it's ugly, will I know it is ugly?"

"Will it be a boy or a girl?"

"Will we be good parents?"

"Will my baby be healthy?"

"Am I eating the right things?"

"Are we financially ready for this?"

"Do we have enough support?"

And let's not forget the baby naming. I have yet to meet a dad who didn't try to name their child after themselves. After telling my husband for the millionth time, our child will not be a junior because almost every Junior I know doesn't go by their first name but a nickname or middle name, we start coming up with a list of real possible names.

I'd like to say the fear stops after you give birth, but it doesn't. It's normal to experience different emotions, but don't get trapped in the fear phase because it will only consume you, especially if you are a person of color giving birth to a Black or Brown baby. Remember, your baby will be beautiful even if many people will choose to see him or her as a threat. This realization can be discouraging at times. Despite the highs and lows, our journey to becoming parents began with joy. My husband and I prayed constantly and surrounded ourselves with positive people and other parents who were giving birth to beautiful Black/Brown babies. This dulled some of the fear and helped quell the fear we were alone or that our baby would grow up alone in a cruel world.

Pregnancy

I have a consistent and predictable menstrual cycle, so when my period was three days late, I knew I was pregnant. At the time, my husband and I had only been married for a little over half a year, and we weren't trying to get pregnant, but we weren't trying not to get pregnant either.

I went to the neighborhood Walgreens and bought a pregnancy kit, the one with two tests in it. Without telling my husband, who was in our bedroom at the time, I went into the bathroom and took the test. I kid you not, as soon as a drop of my urine hit the test, it instantly turned positive.

"Babe," I called his name. He didn't answer, of course. "Babe?" I yelled louder.

I walked out of the bathroom into a three-foot by four-foot area that we call a hallway and looked at Kalen. He had on grey sweatpants and no shirt.

"Babe," I said in total shock and disbelief. I held up the pregnancy test and showed it to him. He immediately smiled and mirroring my disbelief said, "Noooo."

"Babe."

We continued like that for about two more rounds. We finally stood looking at each other in a state of shock, before I finally said it.

"I'm pregnant."

At my first OBGYN appointment with my doctor asked me if I had any questions. My chest began to tighten and I could not fight the tears from rushing down my cheeks. "Did you know that one in four Black women die or have complications giving birth?" My lungs struggled to get oxygen as the pain of fear built up in me. I balled my hands into fists and wiped the tears away as if I were a baby. I tried to push out a few more words but couldn't.

"Oh sweety, you are completely right to feel that way" my OBGYN turned her chair all the way towards me and rolled up to the foot of the bed. "You have some anxiety and fear built up because of that." She states and I nod my head in aggrievance. "But you know that's because often medical officials neglect them, or don't hear them out, but we will not do that here. We are fully committed to hearing you without making assumptions. Is it okay if I also make a note on your file saying that you feel this way?"

I nod again because although my crying has stopped, I still have the tightening in my chest.

"Okay, good." She turns any begins typing on her computer, also allowing me to get my emotions together before turning back to me. "I want you to know Asia, that I will not let that happen, okay." I shake my head and smile.

"Thank you," I breathe, "I was just a little nervous."

"And that is completely valid and it sucks that we live in a world that would make you even feel this way. You let me know if there is anything I can do for you and in the meantime focus on you and the baby and your happiness." She smiled before wrapping up the rest of the appointment and sending the nurse back in to see me out.

My pregnancy was easy in that I wasn't sick all that much. I was a little nauseous in the beginning. One day, when my friends and I went to Red Robin, I thought I would throw up my guts after drinking only water but thankfully I didn't. The burger aroma must have triggered something because I kept gagging, and my food hadn't even arrived. Thankfully, by the time I was three months pregnant, I was feeling fine.

In the first three to four months of pregnancy, you deal with many not-so-enjoyable physical and hormonal changes. On the flip side, it's an exciting time because you get to decide who you will share this fantastic news and whether or not you want to know the sex of your baby before it's born.

We decided to find out the gender of our baby in advance. So, I sent the lab results to my best friends who helped my little sister coordinate a gender reveal for us. After we discovered we were having a boy, which I had a feeling we were, Kalen and I took a trip to Jamaica when I was five months pregnant. We were enjoying our vacation until I received a call from the doctor's office informing me mine was a high-risk pregnancy and that I needed to see a specialist. I cried when I heard the news.

I was so afraid of losing my baby, and I wasn't told exactly how high-risk I was. It wasn't until later that I found out that I had a short cervix. In other words, instead of a brick wall keeping my baby from coming out before his due date, I had a piece of paper that could give at any moment. I was told I would need to go to monthly checkups to monitor the process of my short cervix and my baby, which included strangers sticking their tools and fingers up my vagina to check and see if my cervix was still closed. Around the second appointment, the doctors found that not only was my cervix short, but it was actually shrinking, and my baby was not developed enough to be birthed prematurely. "It looks like your cervix has gotten shorter since the last time we saw you and, to just make sure that the baby stays put and cooking inside you until he is fully done, I'm going to have you take some medicine to hopefully make sure that your cervix does not shrink anymore, okay." The doctor said.

"Okay," I whisper, still trying to breathe because I know if I do anything more than a whisper I will burst into tears. I take a couple more breaths before asking, "So, will this medicine make my cervix grow back to normal?"

"Well, unfortunately we can't make your cervix longer, but it should prevent it from getting any shorter." I went home and began taking the medicine with the fear of my baby falling out of me before he was fully developed and me having to hold me baby in my arms with no warmth or life. A month passed filled with prayer and tears when I arrived at my next appointment. The nurse went through the normal procedure and check before pausing while looking at the screen. "Hmmm, interesting. That's good," She smiled at me while still looking at the screen.

"What?" I asked nervously and a little excited. "Well, the medicine seems to have worked because your cervix is back to its original size, in fact it is slightly longer." I want to bust out in tears and leap for joy, but I still had this person's tools in my body, so I just smiled and breathed a sigh of relief.

"Thank you, God," I whispered.

Giving birth

I'm a high school teacher, and basketball and track coach. I worked until just a few days before I was expected to give birth.

The day I went into labor I was at basketball practice, and my brother was there helping out. We were practicing on the main gym floor, which has three courts surrounded by light gray brick walls and wooden bleachers. Practice was almost over, and the girls were taking a water break when, for some reason, I had the urge to run. I wanted to see how fast I could run even though I was coming up on eleven days before my due date.

"Race me." I say to my brother. But, of course, he refuses and walks away. "Come on, JoJo, are you scared a pregnant lady is going to beat you,"

He rolls his eyes at me, but somehow, I manage to get him to agree to follow through on my absurd challenge. I'm so determined to race him, when I say "Go!" I sprint out as if I'm jumping off of imaginary blocks. Immediately after my first two steps I feel pressure in my vagina and pelvis. It feels like I tore something, but I shrug it off and continue running to the brick wall of the gym. "Oh, that hurts," I limp and almost wobble away to the bleachers.

"Are you okay?" My brother asks me with genuine concern.

"Yeah, I'm good. Why would you make me race you?" I tease him.

"See Asia, that's why I said no." He rolled his eyes and shook his head. I laugh before reassuring him that I was fine a couple more times; little did I know.

I feel pain, but only when I walk, and it isn't actual pain, more a discomfort. After practice, Kalen and I go to watch his little sister play basketball. When we get to the school, I waddle in and the lady at the door looks at me and says, "I hope you're not about to give birth to that baby right now?"

"I have eleven more days left," I say and laugh. After the game, we go home. It's 11:45 pm, when I go to the bathroom and instead of urine feel a rush of fluid pour out of me. I don't think anything of it go back to bed. I wake up not long after and notice more fluids leaked out of me. I go back to the bathroom, and yet another gush of fluid comes out. I turn my eyebrows up and tilt my head to the side. I feel mild period cramps, and then it dawns on me. This could be labor! I call my mom and ask her what it feels like to have my water break. She tells me if my water broke, I should just go to the hospital and check for and time my contractions.

"Babe," I call Kalen in the other room. He jumps up, rubs his eyes.

"Yeah, you okay?"

"I think my water broke, and my mom said we should go to the hospital to make sure." He doesn't seem to grasp what I'm saying, but he starts moving and rummaging through things. I time my contractions while he gets dressed. When I look at my phone, I'm shocked to see they're about three minutes apart. I remember the doctor saying I didn't need to go to the hospital unless my contractions were at least five minutes apart. Kalen comes into the living room where I'm sitting and asks if we should pack a bag?

"I think the baby is coming now."

He stares at me in disbelief. "Well, shoot, let's go then."

It's 1:00 AM when we hop into the car, and the whole way to the hospital, we're laughing because I'm not in pain. We're convinced the doctor is probably going to send us back home.

At the hospital, a nurse examines me and confirms my water did break. The reality of what's happening still hasn't hit me even as contraction sensors are placed on my belly. With every contraction the nurse looks from me to the monitor and lets me know how well I'm handling it. She almost has me convinced I could give birth naturally.

Then the doctor comes in she introduces herself. She seems like a kind lady. When she inserts two fingers to examine how far dilated I am, I feel an indescribable shock of pain. It felt like she was trying to rip me apart with her bare hands.

That's when I remember I was set on an epidural. When she's done examining me, she informs me I am seven centimeters dilated.

"So does that mean I'm in labor?"

"Uh yeah, we need to put you in another room ASAP," she says with a laugh.

Meanwhile, Kalen is on the phone with my dad, and he's relaying the information as they are giving it to us. When Kalen tells my dad, I am 7 cm, I can hear his voice, through the phone "Seven centimeters!!!"

The nurse informs me I may not be able to get an epidural because my labor is progressing so quickly, but I tell her I still want it.

In the Labor & Delivery room, a few nurses are setting it up and our nurse informs the others I am seven centimeters going on eight. All eyes turn to me as if shocked at how calm I seem. I smile and whisper to Kalen, "I still want my epidural." At eight centimeters, they administer it and not long after, my parents and siblings arrive just as I feel a sudden urge to poop.

I don't know if the epidural just isn't very strong or if it takes time to kick in, but I still felt a lot while giving birth, but it didn't hurt.

My baby boy, Judah Rhodes finally arrived at 6:40 am. Kalen and I are officially parents. On TV the childbirth experience is played out so differently than what I experienced. When I look at my baby, I'm tired and happy he's safe and that everything seemed to go so well, but I'm shocked when I don't feel an immediate rush of emotion for him. While I did form a bond with Judah during the pregnancy and while I've already chosen to love him for the rest of his life, I don't yet realize I need time before I can feel what I thought I would feel after his birth. As I soon learn, it is the daily rituals of caring for him and getting to know him that create the deep emotional connection I want to feel.

Breastfeeding

Breastfeeding can be a beautiful experience, but for some, it's painful, and for others, it's not something they want to do or can do. I can breastfeed and the pain I felt in the beginning wasn't too awful. I say this because too many mothers hear the horror stories about breastfeeding. My son latched right away, but it felt uncomfortable for about ten days, then it was fine. For some of my friends and family, that was not the case. They described the pain of breastfeeding as excruciating. Every woman is different, and if the breastfeeding journey is not for you or it's more painful for you, do not feel shame in changing to a bottle or going to formula. You do what you can do and what you want to do for yourself and your baby. Now that my son's teeth are coming in, let me tell you, breastfeeding has gotten a little more intense. I planned on stopping after a year, but so far, it's going well. I believe breastfeeding has helped create an indescribable bond between us. And while I give him countless hugs and kisses, they never seem to be enough. Having a baby has been one of the best experiences.

Mama Bear

In my short time as a mom, I've experienced love and fear unlike any other. Judah, my son, is beautiful and innocent and perfect. I just want him to be happy and healthy. Yes, I check on him during the night or while he naps to make sure he is still breathing, and I know some people say it's because he's my first, but I don't care. I love him so much I can't even describe it. The fear, in the beginning, seemed like it was just as intense as my love. I feared losing him. I had already grown so attached to him while he was in my body, but once he cried out after being born, I vowed at that moment to protect him and love him more than anything.

However, I became overprotective, and viewed everything around him as a potential threat (although I don't think that that should be considered "overprotective," maybe just protective). I thought I understood that nothing comes between a mother and her kids. I thought I understood when my mom would say she didn't care if anyone said anything to her, but if they say something to or about her children, that was different. I honestly couldn't grasp what my mother meant or what she was feeling, until now.

Babies cry

I know that's what they do, but it doesn't change the fact that I don't want to hear my baby cry. When he does, I want to cuddle him and kiss him, so he laughs and smiles or goes to sleep. Even though I know what each cry is for now, and I know when he's just faking it because he wants me to pick him up, I still give in. Yes, he's trained me well, I will be the first to admit it, but I promise, as soon as he can communicate with words, things will change, *hopefully*. I mean, I can hear all the experienced moms laughing at me, but it's okay. I will learn, eventually.

Discussion Questions

1. Which were the best moments of your pregnancy? Why?

2. Did you enjoy your birthing experience? Did you have a birthing plan? What was it? Did it go the way you planned?

3. If you could change anything about your pregnancy experience that you had control over, what would it be? Why?

4. Did you cry when the baby was finally born?

5. Who did you have in the room and why?

CHAPTER SIX

FIRST-TIME PARENTS

FIRST-TIME PARENTS

Having a kid makes you a mother,
but not a great mom.
It might make you a father,
but not a great dad.

It's not just given and accepted.

Those sloppy lips mistaken for kisses,
first time birthday wishes.
Gas mistaken for laughter.
Giggles for days undeserved.
Are not given but earned.

I see you trying your best,
but he keeps crying.
Breastfeeding hurts,
but you're smiling.
'cause it don't get better than this.

WORTHY OF LOVE

Say it's your first time,
Keep 'em speaking'
Fools disguised think they wise
your methods they don't believe in.
But they don't see what you're seeing
'cause that bassinet don't work.
And a little shower for a baby never hurt.
Just keep it pushin' with a little smirk.

But then the moon comes up
and all sanity is lost,
no-one told us that for love, sleep is the cost.
Darkness penetrates beneath your eyes
as you struggle to keep them open.
Holding on to your baby for dear life is your only way
    of coping.
Your goal for that moment and for the next few months
is to just make it to tomorrow while loving your
    little one
a little more and more each day.
Congrats you have made it to the first stage
of having a little babe.

Parenting as a married couple

Before I dive into this, I want first to say that anyone who raises their kids without the help of a spouse, that is truly incredible. This includes people who are married or in a relationship, but your significant other is not helping you with the day-to-day needs of your child. Parenting is a lot of work. I want to avoid saying words like difficult or challenging because sometimes they can be deterrents from having kids or misinterpreted because they are subjective. What I might find easy can be extremely difficult for someone else, and vice versa. So, to maintain a point of clarity, I will try to avoid such terms.

Sleep

It takes a lot of time and energy to raise a child. As a new mother, I realize that every day. Before I became pregnant, I would get a minimum of eight to ten hours of sleep a night. I never took naps because I didn't need to. I was already receiving the total amount of sleep I needed. After having a child, my sleeping schedule changed completely. It feels like I'm always tired (which I am because my son does not sleep through the night; he is only seven months old). When I say he doesn't sleep through the night, I mean he doesn't go the whole night without wanting to be next to me or comfort feed. At least now it's only once and not several times a night.

Some people like coffee or can't operate without breakfast. I need sleep. I can't work to the best of my ability without it, which is probably most people. Small tasks seem way more complicated than they are, and motivation tends to plummet quickly. Of course, the most significant recommendation for avoiding sleep deprivation is "sleep when the baby sleeps" (*rolls eyes). I have too many things to do, people to see, and places to go. No, really, I've tried in the past to do that. However, I'm usually worked up from trying to put my child to sleep, and I often want to relax, but my relaxation is not taking a nap.

Breaking all the "rules"

Many suggestions seem like parenting rules. Another suggestion is on how to bathe your child. They say to only have 3 inches of water in the tub, and to use your sink or bathtub. Yeah, that didn't work for us. My son gets baths, but it is so much easier to shower him with us while we shower, and it is far more convenient.

The most important lesson learned from breaking the bathing rule is the phrase, "We tried it, and it does not work for us."

It is entirely okay to try something out, but if you find an easier way that works for you, then you do that. Not everyone can or will parent the same way. We all can't be perfectly vegan and have four nannies and pediatricians in our home. Not saying bathing your child is complicated, but there are ways to get the job done without causing harm to the child and still making it a pleasant experience.

With that being said, it is difficult for others to understand that there are multiple ways of parenting, and many parents will feel like their way of parenting is the best. That's fine until they try to force their way of parenting on other people. What helps is to be open minded, listen to suggestions but always do what works best for you and your family.

Because I only have one child, and he is a boy, it might not be taken the same way, but how we care for your child's hair can be interesting in the Black community. I say interesting because it wasn't until recently, like within the last five to eight years, our natural hair has become more widely accepted, both socially and even in the beauty world. I know there will be suggestions about how to style my son's hair that might sound strange or I may even disagree with, and others I may really like and want to try.

Little Victories

Making your child laugh or not think about a toy they believe they can't live without is a small victory. Having some alone time in your day and breathing is a small victory, the list goes on and on. The point is, those small moments should be celebrated. Parents are often so hard on themselves that we forget to recognize when things are going well. Even if you have one small victory a day or even one a week, it is important to celebrate those moments so you can keep on keeping on.

You will probably hear this a lot, but it's true. Enjoy the little moments because time goes by so fast, especially when you're sleep-deprived and hanging on by a thread. The days blur together, and before you know it, your newborn is babbling, feeding himself, and crawling, or rolling over.

Babysitting

Do not feel pressured to let someone babysit your kids just because they ask or because they're family. Remember that just because someone has kids, family, or is friendly does not mean they need to have your kids under their supervision.

If you do agree to let someone babysit, make a list of things that you want them to do when watching your child, and if you feel like they will not follow it, then it's most likely because it's your mom babysitting your child, be prepared to hear the "grandmother knows best," line.

Find people you are comfortable with and good with babies or kids that are the same age as your child. Someone can be good with teenagers, but they are terrible with infants. Keep this in mind because sometimes we don't even know what strengths or weaknesses are when it comes to babysitting. Also, if it's been years since someone has been around an infant or toddler giving them a refresher on what to do is okay. If they feel like you are extra cautious, so be it. As a new parent, it is almost impossible not to be labeled as being or doing more than needed. What worked for me was starting with smaller amounts of time and gradually adding more. That's how I became more comfortable leaving my son with his grandparents.

Putting a hold on things

When I got married and then later became pregnant, I would hear a lot of people say, "Now, you have to put your dreams on hold," or "No more traveling for you guys," and it was annoying because marriage and starting a family does not have to stop your dreams or defer them. You can still travel if you want to with a baby. My husband and I were going to, but then Covid-19 happened. You can still strive to achieve your dreams, in whatever time frame you want to achieve them. You can reach them.

Everyone is different, and sometimes others project their fears onto you. If you're reading this and feel like this might be directed towards you as an insult, I want you to know that couldn't be further from the truth. As parents, we do what we believe to be the best things for our children based on what we know now; there is nothing wrong with not pursuing a dream IF THAT IS WHAT YOU WANT TO DO! But you don't have to just because you become a parent. This can be debated, but at the end of the day, nobody knows your capacity, talent, and drive like you. Nobody but God and you know what you can achieve.

Oops

You will mess up as a parent, and you will do it more than once, possibly every day. Get used to it. We should never settle, but be careful of making it an unhealthy obsession and not giving yourself grace when it comes to the fact that no-one is a perfect parent.

When Judah was just a few months old, he had a hernia. After checking Web MD and scrolling on Google, which

I would NOT recommend, especially to a first-time mom (if you have questions, just call a professional or the advice nurse), I immediately scheduled an appointment with the pediatrician and went into his bedroom, watched him sleep, and balled my eyes out because I somehow thought it was my fault.

We went to the appointment and the doctor went over the notes the nurse had taken when checking us in. "So, you think your baby has a hernia?" She asked while looking at her computer. "Yeah, at least that's what his symptoms seem to show me."

"Well, you are correct. He does have a hernia and, most of the time these will go away on their own." She continued to talk about what we should do if any other symptoms might show, which could lead to something more serious, while explaining how he will be okay. Her words were comforting, especially to know that, not only was my baby fine and would get better without any surgery, but also knowing that I didn't fail him as a mother in anyway was nice to hear. Then, when Judah hit his head for the first time, I thought I was the worst mom on the planet. He cried, then stopped and was fine only to hit his head again a few days later. I told my mom, and she and some other moms assured me that all of their kids had bumped their heads at some point and survived.

In short, continue to learn and do your best. When all else fails, love your child. My mom always tells me you can't spoil someone with love, and I agree. Love your baby with every ounce of your being, and hopefully, one day, they will love you too. Usually by the time they finally realize you are more than just a walking/talking boob.

Discussion Questions

1. What do you like the most about parenting?

2. Are you about to become a parent or are you currently a parent? What were some fears you have/had? Have you overcome them and how?

3. What did you name your child and why? How did you choose their name?

4. What was the weirdest piece of advice you received on parenting? What is one of your odd parenting tricks?

5. How would you describe your parenting style in three words or less?

CHAPTER SEVEN

FAMILY

A HEALTHY FAMILY

The other day I was thinking,
why do we talk to strangers, social media friends,
    clients and maybe even friends,
but we don't speak to our real people?
Our family?
Why don't we put energy into having these
    conversations with
our spouse, siblings, parents, cousins, aunties and
    uncles and even grandparents?

I'm at a loss for words.

Because how dare I?
How can I put energy and effort into
trying to understand and
trying to heal and mend a broken relationship with a
    stranger
before starting with my own blood?

I'm trying to prevent everyone else's ships from
   sinking —
my own ship is sinking —
because I got leaks that I'm not tending to.
Broken board that needs to be patched or replaced to
   start anew.
Parts of my ship need to be updated but I'm so concerned about updating other people's ships.

In fact, I don't even think that's it.
I think it's because my dysfunctional ship,
still floats,
it still moves and
So, I fear that fixing it will make people angry, that is
   the members of my crew.
Changing it will cause more chaos,
And what if I make changes and now my ship sinks
   because the changes were too much?
What if my crew hates me? And I mess up.

It's a conversation that goes on in our head.
We fear healing.
No, we fear hurting,
but you learn in first aid that
you cannot make matters worse.
But instead of taking a risk to save a life
we fear we will take it by helping
so, we choose to let it slowly die.

FAMILY

But I refuse to let it, fear, control me.
I refuse to let relationships slowly end
and claim we grew apart
so, I don't have to have a heart-to-heart.

The bottom line…
if I claim I ride for my family
I can't settle for matching pajamas happy,
when we disconnected and crying
so before other families are fine
I need to first see to mine.

Difficult conversations

In college, my grandma and I have another talk about race. However, this time, I am not shocked when my grandma explains what she was taught to perceive as right during her time.

"What are you talking about? You have Black children and grandchildren! You need to understand this!" I scream at the top of my lungs. My eyes were red from built-up frustration. And my cheeks were wet with tears. I stared at my grandma, waiting for a response.

"I just don't know Asia," she said as she looks back at me with her flushed face and teary eyes.

"You see, Asia, I was taught not to see color, and that was supposed to show that everyone's the same, that we are equal."

"Yes, grandma, I understand you were taught that, but we ARE different. And if you can't see how our stories are different or how society treats us differently, then you are saying you don't acknowledge my experience or the inequities that I or people who look like me have to endure."

"Oh, I never thought of it that way." She sits and thinks for a second, "That was not my intention Asia, I have a lot to learn."

We both are emotionally drained, and our eyes burned from the conversation, but I finally breathed a sigh of relief. Most of our conversations about racial equality usually begin and end with crying, yelling, and frustration. But at the end of each conversation, we both still have the desire to never give up on one another's perspective. The last part is critical. You see, I love my grandma more than anything, and I can tell you that my grandma feels the same way about me. We both want to understand why the other person thinks the way they think while at the same time wanting to gain new insight and perspectives of our own.

Although our conversations are difficult and uncomfortable, we both know we need to have them. We share more than raw emotions and frustrations; we also share our thoughts and feelings. We also move beyond understanding and into practicing better responses and actions.

"I want to learn, to understand, and to continue to grow. I know I'm not as young as I used to be, but I don't want to hurt the ones I love even if it is unintentionally. It's just hard and frustrating when you think you are learning something for good and to make things right, but it's still wrong and you are hurting the very ones you love," Her eyes are puffy and red. She's not looking at me but off into the distant. She is gripping the blanket she has covering her as if she is trying to grab the past by its throat, angry with the confusion and pain it has caused us. "This is not easy you know?" she tries to regain control over her breathing.

She is right though. It is not easy to be taught one thing and then be told that everything you have learned is a lie. It is not easy to love someone as if they were the air you breathe, then learn they feel hurt by words or actions you did not realize would hurt them. It is not easy and as I think about it while my grandma calms herself, I think about my own actions. *So, I was to believe that I shouldn't have thought before I spoke, calmed my nerves, and approached my grandma in a way of growing our relationship instead of coming from a place of hurt and anger. But how blessed I was that she loved me nonetheless and my words and pain did not fall upon deaf ears but those of someone who wants to know not just my success, or pain but how we can be better in the future.*

"I'm sorry, Grandma. I got so angry and surprised at what I was hearing that I didn't stop to think about how what I was saying might impact you or how you feel. Sorry for snapping at you. Despite my emotions, there is a better way of communicating more calmly." My own breathing has calmed as I looked at the most beautiful women on earth in her oversized cream robe with a gray blanket resting on top of her while her feet are inclined on the floral lazy boy. If the world will never understand my story, or strangers would never see my pain to truly understand my success and my identity I will be okay, but if this woman sitting before me, who has changed my diapers, wiped my tears, picked me up from school, fed me, bathed me and has loved me unconditionally, I would be a wreck. How can our relationship continue to grow if the ones I hold closest to my heart and love me do not also recognize my suffering or know my story?

I want our relationship to continue to grow and blossom as we learn about each other. I don't wish to stop learning or to become strangers who only share blood and holiday cheer. I want us to grow like wildfire even as we grow old, schedules change and visiting looks different. I continue looking at my grandma and can't help but smile.

Both my grandma and I point out things we need to work on, and she promises to engage in the uncomfortable work with race and equity. She realizes that just having Black children or grandchildren does not mean she cannot have racist tendencies.

I believe the only reason we have been able to have these conversations is that we are both open to being vulnerable and making changes. The main reason, however, is that we genuinely love each other so much!

We never once think we will need to cut each other off or that our relationship will end because we know that this relationship will take work, and it is and will always be worth it. We are not perfect, but we strive to be our best because of our love.

When a controversial event or issue happens, it's easy to take to social media with a desire to share my perspective in hopes of enlightening people. This is because there isn't the anxiety of face-to-face communication, nor do I know the people online, so I and many other human beings behind the keyboard may feel more inclined to risk the relationship of a stranger than that of a family member or close friend. When I say risk, I don't mean trolling someone, but engaging in what may be a difficult discussion, but online without the emotional strain and fear of ruining a relationship if we find out that we do not agree. I should say that I do not actually go on other people's pages and comment under their post about controversial topics nor do I post click bait to troll, but it can feel easier to do these things, which is why I have found myself erasing a lot of comments without posting.

The fear of realizing you have different views, or you might disagree with someone you grew up with, can be scary sometimes. This can make it feel more difficult to address those same issues within my own household or with family members.

However, with family, it's different. There is the fear of losing a family member, even if you're maintaining a toxic relationship or stunting the growth of someone who is related to you by blood. What am I holding onto if someone I love is lost or not evolving in their thinking? Why refuse to have a challenging conversation when I love them unconditionally despite the disagreements we may have? I didn't want to ruin my relationship with my grandma and even though it took a lot of uncomfortable conversations, my relationship with her has deepened.

Before talking to her, I created a thousand reasons in my head why I couldn't say certain things to her because she is my grandma. How do I tell someone I love and that loves me they say stuff that hurts me? However, I am her granddaughter. If she is to have a conversation about changing mentality or a specific behavior from anyone, it should be from someone she loves, someone who knows and sees her as more than any mistake or judgment she might have. "Grandma, you know I love you more than anything right?" We had just been having an intense conversation and I noticed a shift in her body language.

"What? Oh, I know Asia, but thank you for saying that because I know you're not my baby, but I see you like my daughter, so you are my baby, and it can be hard hearing that as a parent I messed up. I don't want you to resent me for that." Her shoulders relax as she takes a deep breath and exhales any worries she might have had, giving us more space and opportunity to grow instead of question if our love for each other is at stake.

"Grandma I could never resent you," I laugh and the mood lightens. After seeing my grandma's reaction, I am taught, yet

FAMILY

once again, the importance of communicating from a place of love and desire to educate and grow instead of a place of pain and anger. It is more rewarding and beneficial to both sides this way. Although we love each other and know we will always love each other, in the heat of the moment doubt can creep up, so it is important for us to remind others of our love.

We also want to understand each other. I would ask questions like, "Grandma, how could you not believe they murdered him for being Black because he literally had no weapon?" I asked really confused on why she didn't understand what I was saying.

"Asia, the police could not get away with something like that because that is just so bad. So, clearly, he must have done something wrong." She explained completely believing in our justice system.

"Grandma, you are assuming that every cop is a saint and we have a perfect justice system that believes in equality. Plus, did you not see the video? He had his hands up there was no need to murder him. Nothing will justify them shooting him while he wasn't a threat with his hands up, nothing. They are police and their jobs are to protect, not be the voice of life and death." My frustration is starting to build up and I know I become more reactive when I let my emotions get the best of me, so I focus on my breathing.

"I see that, and I get it, but I just don't understand how, in America, our police would do such a thing. We have grown so much from those times. They wouldn't allow that to happen." She was still trying to understand how something like this could happen and then it dawned on me. My grandma was not trying to defend the police officers who were in the wrong or justify murder, but she truly wanted to believe that our system of justice was, in fact, just. This gave me relief because, again, I realized her desire to see the good in our police, which there is definitely good, caused her to dismiss the possibility that there could be some bad.

"Grandma, I love how you want to see the good in everyone, but we're not perfect and there are people out there who still do not believe in equality out there."

"Really, in this day and age? Well, how do they even get to become police?" She asked genuinely trying to understand. If I did not breathe and hear my grandma out, I could have thought she was still trying to convince me that all police were just and good, but I knew better. I knew she was actually trying to understand why the America she believed in had fallen short of her expectations and that is not an easy pill to swallow.

"Really, but I hope it gets better." I laugh and we end the conversation there for the day. I am not worried of losing my relationship with my grandma because I know I genuinely love her unconditionally. Even if she wanted to give up on me, which is not the case at all, it wouldn't happen because I will never stop loving her, so we could never be broken.

Many times, I wondered how can you know your family loves you? At what age does the love they feel for you change? What causes love to weaken or fade away? I've come to terms with the fact that it doesn't matter. I love my family and it doesn't matter if they love me back because I have chosen to love them unconditionally despite our differences.

But loving your family unconditionally isn't always easy. There is nothing like family, but even those closest to you can sometimes lift you up or tear you down. I want to focus on how loving unconditionally can help create a healthy family. You must begin with yourself before you can aim to have a healthy relationship with your family. Are you healthy? To be healthy, do you need to resolve something? Does healing yourself require resolving an issue with a loved one or do you need to seek counseling with God and/or a professional therapist? After you have reflected on your own needs, you can go back to focusing on the family unit.

There is no perfect family. We all make mistakes. Take some time to determine each family member's strengths and areas for improvement. Now, just as there is no perfect family, there is also no perfect order to any of the steps I will mention next. Every family is different and experiencing different challenges. What I share with you is less of a solution and more of a suggestion. I'm sharing what has worked for my family in the hopes you can see if any of these practices will work for you.

How well do you know your family members? When was the last time you talked to them? When talking with my grandma, it was easier because we spoke almost every week anyway, and, before college, I was going to her house to stay overnight every other weekend. I ask these questions because sometimes we assume we know a family member just because they're a family member, but we don't truly know what they've been through or are going through. They could be facing a trauma you aren't aware of, or struggling with mental health, drugs, alcohol, spiritually, or insecurities. Maybe they have yet to address the issue or seek help for it.

Before you can address issues you're having with a family member, you have to assess their health needs. If your family member is not healthy and/or in a state of mind that can sustain a conversation focused on resolution, you will just waste your time. Keep in mind you are not diagnosing your family members. You may not be licensed or skilled enough to do such a thing. It's possible they may not want to share some of their personal issues with you for any number of reasons. That alone creates another challenge.

I recently struggled with learning how to unconditionally love a family member while only being able to watch from a distance.

"I'm dropping out of college." My brother says before looking at me and waiting for my response.

"What?!"

"I'm not going back to college."

"You mean you're taking a break? Like you're just overwhelmed and need a break, or . . ." I don't finish the words because I don't want to plant any ideas in his head that might not be there yet, but it's too late.

"Like I'm no longer going to be in college, Asia. I just feel it is not my thing right now, and I would rather focus on something I love, which is music."

I sit there dumbfounded before I try to explain he can do both. "Bro, you realize you can go to college and do music still. I mean aren't you doing that now?"

I pause to allow him to respond

"I mean yeah, but it's different," He sighs as if I am missing something.

"College is hard now because you are still trying to get the hang of things and you still have to take classes that you may not be interested in. Just push through," I begin but feel like I am forcing him through torture because this is the only way I was taught. What I didn't realize at the time was that I was just projecting my own fear and lack of knowledge onto him. I can tell by the way he's looking at me he has already made up his mind.

"Asia, I already made the decision and called. I just wanted to let you know." My jaw drops, and I can't find the words to say. I'm irritated but mostly scared, and I can't imagine how my parents feel at this moment.

"Did you tell Mom and Dad?" "Yeah, they weren't happy." "Yeah, I bet."

"They just don't understand. Like, this is what I was made to do, and if I can spend a hundred percent of my time on music versus only a third of my time, imagine how much better I would be." He's been thinking about this for a while, and there is nothing I can say that will change his mind. I look at my husband for support or advice in trying to persuade him, but he just tilts his head and shrugs.

"Hey, bro, if you feel like this is what you are supposed to do, then we can't argue, but just make sure you aren't just acting on impulse, and you have thought about this."

As my brother and husband talk, I try to focus on my breathing because there are so many thoughts running through my mind. I'm worried. My brother is only nineteen. My parents can't force him to do anything. They can't just tell him to go to school and do what they say. That would only hurt their relationship. I'm worried, not because I don't believe in my brother's dreams (because I do), but dropping out of college in America as a young Black man makes him no different than any stereotype society already has of him. Before being a college dropout, he was an intelligent young man going to college and now . . . My brother is smart. I take a deep breath. He is talented. I inhale deeper and then release. God still watches over him, so why am I so worried?

Kalen and my brother stop talking, and we hug JoJo and pray for him. In the car on the way home, I can't help but think about the thoughts that have been dancing, more like raging in my head. Why am I so worried? Is it because I know he is still a kid? Or is it because of the dark bags underneath his eyes, his skinny body drowning in clothes that used to fit him, and his lips blackened by constant smoking? No, I am worried because I have seen students and family members and friends pursue their dreams and fall short and I don't want the same to become a reality for my brother. But it is within that same thought that I feel guilty for even doubting my brother that, for him choosing his dreams over other people's desires or plans for his life, is success in itself. However, I am his older sister and still can't help but worry.

It's different when you encourage someone else and when you pray for someone else's family. It's scarier when it's your own sibling. I take a breath as I realize my brother is deciding what feels best for his life. Why am I trying to force him onto a path that is comfortable *for me*? Is it because it's the path I took? But we're not the same, and I shouldn't be doing that. When we get home, Kalen and I revisit the conversation we had with my brother and finally agree that the only next step is to continue to love my brother. Loving someone, whether they choose your suggested path and when they have their demons to battle, can feel as though you are on the other side of an invisible wall, in which they can't honestly see or hear you. All you can do is watch from the sidelines and hope they won't be led astray or have to endure harsh challenges along the way. We care, hope, and pray they will make it through okay. Showing up consistently and offering our love, no matter the challenges someone has to face, is the hardest thing about loving our family unconditionally.

A year or so passes, when my brother goes on a mission trip to Africa with my parents. When he returns, we can tell he has discovered what it means to be himself and to have a purpose. There is a new air about him. His eyes seem to focus on what is right in front of him, and even his skin is brighter. He shares his experiences and tells us about how Africa changed him, and how his relationship with God has deepened. Over the next couple of years, my brother gets back to a healthy weight, stops smoking, works on his music, and pursues what seems to be a journey focused on self-discovery.

If I have made this sound very simple, I want to clarify that it is not simple. If a family member decides to let you in and help them with anything they're attempting to resolve, support them, but enlist the help of a trained professional.

Let's talk about issue resolution when it pertains to an action a loved one took. Maybe you don't agree with the action they took, or it wasn't polite, discriminatory, etc. You have to be honest, but remember to address the action, not the individual. The action is terrible, but the individual is not. People shut down when you try to paint a picture of them as an evil monster. They go into defense mode and no longer listen but instead try to prove to you why they're not, in fact, inherently evil. Also, assess yourself; why are you upset? Are you in the mental state required for this kind of conversation? Or are you angry?

Have you prayed? Prayed for your family member? For yourself? For the relationship? It would help if you honestly started with prayer but as I noted there is no perfect order for any of this. We can only do so much as a family member and not an expert (assuming we aren't an expert in giving family therapy). Family conversations tend to go best when five people are not disagreeing with one person, but when there is one-on-one communication. In this way no one ever feels like they are being attacked by the people closest to them.

What do you want the end goal to be? How can you best get there? Know that whatever you're going to meet to discuss might be uncomfortable. To put it frankly, no one human being has the power to change anyone. Only we can decide to change, and change doesn't happen overnight. Below are some topics that might come up when attempting to address issues with family:

1. Mental health
2. Sexual abuse
3. Religion/Beliefs
4. Respect
5. Inside jokes/language
6. Physical health
7. Race/racism and equality
8. Abuse
9. Struggles/hardships
10. Old drama (smaller groups with involved people only)

However, before you can even dive into these conversations, you need to make sure you are prepared to have these conversations. Is the environment safe for everyone? What are some ground rules you feel need to be made to create a safe environment for discussion and growth? Write them down as a family, share them and follow them.

Some suggestions:

1. Stay on topic
2. Remain silent while others are speaking
3. Listen to understand and not only to respond
4. Have an open mind
5. Check your body language
6. Be okay with being uncomfortable
7. Let everyone speak

These are just a few, but they come up a lot. First, you want to be clear about family rules, so if anyone has questions about them, be prepared to unpack them. This way nothing is left to interpretation.

Of course, the next step is to meet with your family member(s). You may even want to choose a facilitator, timekeeper, or someone who can reinforce the rules.

Know that conversation is not the only way to address and resolve issues especially when it may have to deal with an extreme problem or abuse is involved. In those cases, bring in the professionals.

Keep in mind that the desire to have these conversations can dwindle when they are not managed with unconditional love. These conversations can lead to the development of healthy relationships. It is one way to give those you care about enough space to grow, and it gives us space to step back and accept our loved ones for who they are and not who we're trying to make them be. Loving family without condition reminds us to love, not because of the relationship but because we want to establish healthy boundaries.

Extended Family & In-Laws

Like our immediate family, siblings, and parents, grace is needed when it comes to our extended family and in-laws. When I got married, and my relationship with my in-laws began, I was nervous because I knew so little about them other than the fact they were related to my husband. Despite my discomfort, I had already committed myself to loving them. I know that sounds strange, but it's how I felt. They loved and supported my husband, and my husband loved them and, to me, that was reason enough. Now I know this is conditional love because I expected them to continue to love my husband and eventually to love me. However, in time, my mindset shifted.

The quickest way for a relationship to fail is to love someone or claim to love someone while setting up conditions as to why you love them. This is especially true if you've set conditions before you really got a chance to know them. How can you love someone you don't know anything about and expect them to love you back? You can't, because if you or they break those conditions, and you decide you are done with loving them, you never truly loved them.

When I first met my in-laws, I loved the idea of having them in my life. The idea of having an extended family was appealing, but I had no idea what that would look like or what to expect. I got to thinking I loved them just because of who they were, but I was scared they wouldn't love me. that, in turn, stunted the growth of our relationship in the beginning. How can a relationship grow if we place countless limitations on it?

Loving unconditionally means showing grace and having patience so a relationship can deepen gradually. I eventually came to understand the different dynamics of my new family. As soon as I took a step back, decided to be patient, and accepted that no one is perfect, especially me, our relationship blossomed. I see my in-laws not my husband's family, but as *my* family. I'm at their home almost every other day. By now, I have developed a deep love for them. I hate calling them in-laws because I feel like it distances them from me. In my time of confusion and wonderment, I was reminded to give grace because we deserve it and be patient so that my unconditional love could begin to set root and grow.

I hope as you are reading this now, you are not trying to rush any relationship. And that you have the patience to consider how amazing having an extended family can be. Though there may be differences in communication or family dynamics, with grace, consistency and unconditional love, relationships not only blossom, but continue to grow.

Discussion Questions

1. What are some conversations you want to have with certain family members? Have you had the conversations? Why or why not?

2. What has been a struggle when dealing with familial issues? Why? What do you plan to do differently?

3. Does "letting go and letting God" mean you are giving up on a family member? What does it mean to you?

4. What is keeping you from engaging with family? What excuses have you made? How have you validated those excuses? Are there some excuses that you need to get rid of? Are some of the reasons legitimate?

CHAPTER EIGHT

MISDIRECTED LOVE

THE DIFFERENCE BETWEEN STRANGERS AND FAMILY

Why do we care so much about strangers?
We prepare for stranger danger
and never uncle, aunt, cousin, sibling, family, or friend
  danger.

I know you are probably not going to like me for
  this, but
did you know every year around 76% of the kids
who are kidnapped
are kidnapped by family?
While 24% are kidnapped by strangers.

Did you know that 93% of sexual offenders know their
  victims?
Most of them, family, friends or acquaintances,
34% of those family
and only 7% being strangers.

WORTHY OF LOVE

Did you know it is far easier to block or delete a
    comment or tweet,
from a stranger rather than someone we know?
And that our kids are not being hurt by strangers,
but by friends and family we think are close?

So why are we preparing children to be careful around
people we have never met before
instead of protecting them from people we think
    we know?!

I'm a little confused.
Is it because we are scared to admit
our family members can be abusers too?
Are we so determined to appear perfect that we are
    indifferent,
in turn choosing the side of the abuser and neglecting
    those abused,
all so we can cover up the truth?
Is it because we can't handle the truth?

I don't understand why we say "don't touch strangers,"
but we force our kids to sit on people's laps.
We tell them even when they are uncomfortable
    with touch
to still give that family member a hug.
We set boundaries and guidelines for people we have
    never met before,
but don't set boundaries for the people who have keys
    to our front door.

MISDIRECTED LOVE

You see, the true difference between strangers and
    family is
that strangers have to try to hurt us
and family members don't.

We know how to handle a stranger, but it's hard for us
    to tell family no.
No, don't touch me!
No, you can't have a hug.
No, you can't come over.
No, that comment was rude.
No, I do not agree with you.
No, I do not want your input or advice.
No, you are not right.
No, you may not watch my kids.
No, this is none of your business.
No, you do not have a say in my relationships.
No, that was inappropriate.
No, you may not do whatever you want to do,
just because you think your so-called title allows
    you to.
I don't care if we grew up together,
if you know my mom,
or we are connected by marriage or blood.
We must accept the difference between strangers and
    family is true.
That family can do more harm than strangers do,
and that's the truth.

Strangers

There have been times when I poured countless hours and energy into non-existent relationships, for the sake of feeling loved and accepted. As an adolescent, I struggled to fit in and be accepted as a friend by some of my peers. Eventually, by being my authentic self I was able to find my voice and the acceptance I longed for. However, when I started college, things changed.

It's my freshman year of college, and I am sitting in a circle with other girls who share my dorm floor. Our RA has asked us to introduce ourselves and give our name, major, and why we decided to attend the university.

"Hello, my name is Asia. I'm a biology major, and I chose this school because I got a full-ride scholarship."

The girl sitting next to me, after she tells us her name and major, lets us know the reason why she is here, at a university that costs around 43,000 dollars a year. "I am here in hopes of getting a ring by spring," She smiles while the other girls in the group all nod their heads and smile as well. I can't stop my eyes from going wide in shock at what she just said. "Yeah," she continues, "It would be nice to make friends, but I really want to leave this whole college experience with a husband." I'm pretty sure my mouth dropped to the floor, and my eyeballs were about to pop out of my head at the ludicrous statement she'd just made. But as I looked around the room, many of the other girls were nodding their heads and smiling in agreement.

It was hard to believe. How could someone be willing to pay $43,000 a year, not to better themselves, but to find a husband? Why not just use a dating site like eHarmony? Or why not get out into the real world and date?

It was only the first week of school and thankfully I was less concerned about making friends than I was about avoiding strange experiences. As it turns out, I had reason for concern.

I was in a general English class discussing the inequalities of the world. The class had about thirty- five students in it all sitting in a U shape facing the teacher and the whiteboard. I was sitting on the side of the U shape closest to the exit of the classroom and the whiteboard. The teacher was speaking about the different challenges and adversities we could write about when she said, "There are many life-changing moments that you can write about. Many authors or writers find inspiration from some of the most challenging parts of their lives. Whether that is inequality, feeling lost, or depression. We live in a world that some can face sexism, racial inequality." As she continued, some side conversation erupted and, before she got into the heart of the creative assignment, we were supposed to create to share a little of who we are, one of my white male peers stood up and declared, "Slavery didn't exist. In fact, this was a voluntary act that happened with the approval from their community," He is referring to the Black/African community. He was a short guy with dirty blond hair that could be confused as brown. He wore a flannel buttoned up all the way to his neck that was tucked into his dad jeans completed with a brown belt. The teacher didn't stop just let him continue as he went on to say more, but my mind was already racing as was my heart rate. I tried my best to sink deep into my chair and disappear. Every day since the beginning of the school year, I was reminded of how different I was from my other students. In most, if not all, of my classes, I was the only Black student and the only person of color. I tried to slow my breathing to calm myself, but as I scanned the room, I found, once again, that the many faces of my peers were nodding in agreement. Although not all of them were, no one challenged him, not even me. I felt paralyzed from the shock of what I'd just heard.

After class, I tried to walk back to my dorm as quickly as possible when I bumped into a friend. Ashley was a sweet girl. She had long hair and loved Jesus with all her heart. Every activity she did, she did with her whole being including worship. During worship, she would praise God, her voice unapologetically the loudest in the room and her hands raised to the heavens as if no one else was in the room was with her. I am as grateful today, as I was then, that I met her.

Ashley asked if I was okay because she noticed something was off and told her what happened in class. She listened intently and was shocked, but her response was, "Really, he said that? Maybe you're mistaken. Or maybe he meant something else."

Although she meant well or intended those words to make me feel better, the impact of hearing them was devastating. The pain built up in my chest, until my lungs struggled to push oxygen throughout my body. Again, someone was saying what I experienced must have been fake, or that I imagined things. I felt alone again.

I thanked her for listening to me and continued to my dorm. Unfortunately, I continue to experience and overhear microaggressions. I can recall remarks such as, "Do you even need sunscreen?"

"Can I go to your church so I can see how Black people dance and do that thing when they shout?"

"Yeah, the Black athletes have a cheat because they're just born ripped." Or one of my favorites, "Can you talk to them with your slang so they will understand?"

Over and over again, I tried to block it all out and focus on why I was there, which was not to make friends but to get a degree. One night, I was pushed over the edge when I received a phone call while walking back to my dorm from my friend's place. The call was about my cousin. He had been jumped and mugged downtown by two white men. I'd had enough. I walked into the coliseum (dang, what is the word, like a stadium outside type place) and screamed at the sky, "Why God? Why?" I dropped onto the grass and held myself while I cried the ugliest cry you could imagine. My body was shaking uncontrollably, and snot was running down my nose as I whispered, "I'm tired, please, why?"

After what seemed like hours of crying, I sat up and stared into the darkness. The air was crisp, and I could see my breath. I closed my eyes, and as I tried to calm myself and slow my breathing, I felt warmth surrounding me, and then words began to fill my head, so I began to write. I wrote without stopping until I produced the poem, "Quiet ole me," a spoken-word piece.

Weeks after I wrote the poem, I was invited to an open mic. I decided to perform it there. The night before, I felt nervous about how the poem would be received. I called my dad and told him I was sure someone was going to kill me after I shared my poem. My dad reassured me that would not happen and wasn't the point of me performing this poem to get over the feeling of being accepted and instead share a message that needed to be heard?

"Asia stop focusing on the negative…"

"But Dad, what if they don't understand?" I interrupted.

"But what if they do?" "What if I mess up?!" "What if you don't?"

"But Dad, what if…" I tried to think of something else.

"Asia, do you believe you should recite this poem?" he asked patiently. "Because if you do, which we both know you do, then stop making excuses and do it."

I agreed and told him I loved him before hanging up the phone. The following night I performed the poem. When they called my name, my whole body was shaking with nervous energy. I had been mulling my lines over and over to myself like a mad person so I could remember them. As I approached the mic, I felt everyone's gaze on me, and I thought I would explode, but I knew this had to be done. I took a deep breath and put on some 3D black frame glasses to indicate I was now in character as… Quiet ole me. I pour every ounce of my soul into my delivery. I could feel only the emotions that belonged to each line of poetry I recited. When I finished, I was back to reality. But it was a different reality. Everyone was on their feet screaming and thanking me for sharing what some of them had long wanted to say or hear. People walked up to me with gratitude because they didn't know someone could feel the way I felt but they needed to hear it. I couldn't help but smile. Speaking my truth was worth the risk of being accepted or rejected because, in the end, all that mattered was I accepted myself.

It's not unusual to be afraid of the unknown or about what others might think about us. Sometimes it's easy to forget to focus on ourselves or on eliminating threats that can come closer to home.

Unconditional love can blind us. We may long for it at the risk of wanting to be loved and accepted by those who do not matter. When it comes to our families, we tend to believe our loved ones have accepted us, so what's the point of nurturing those relationships? The point being we should never neglect our closest relationships.

We want to believe that the people we call family and friends are healthy, and practical and would never do anything to hurt or harm us, but the fact is people, all people, are imperfect and at times can be selfish.

Feel safer addressing a stranger rather than family.

It may seem easier to love a stranger unconditionally because we don't have expectations. What we fail to realize is all new relationships allow us the opportunity to love someone new before they can disappoint us. We set up boundaries in our interactions with strangers because we don't know them well enough. At the same time, we neglect our familial relationships because it takes work and uncomfortable moments to work through issues we need to address.

I'm watching the news when I hear the story of a child abused by a family friend. Immediately, I freeze. I'm in the middle of saying why it's essential to protect ourselves from strangers when I overhear the newscaster say the words again, "Family friend."

The abuser may be a stranger to us, but not to his victim. My mind instantly scans family members as potential threats, and I don't like it, so I stop my thought process. It's in this moment I realize we tend not to think straight when it comes to our own family and friends. There have been countless times when hurtful words or acts were directed at me by strangers. I'm used to being on the lookout for "Stranger Danger" or "mysterious white vans" but not to thinking about which boundaries to set with family members. The fact is rules tend to bend or stretch for people we know because it's hard for us to believe they can be capable of something that will hurt us. Christian Homes and Families Addressing the imperfect aspects within ourselves, family and friends can be uncomfortable and stressful. As Christians, we believe we serve a forgiving God. When we have a situation of hurt, betrayal, or abuse, and those we love ask to be forgiven, we may feel obligated to forgive and forget and leave it at that instead of taking all the necessary actions on our end of a situation.

In the case of sexual abuse within the family, when the abuser admits what they've done and asks for forgiveness, we as Christians may feel there are no other actions on our part that need to be taken. That is wrong. Praying, loving unconditionally, or even forgiving are all awesome, but in a scenario like this, we cannot leave it at that. Of course, the abuser has steps of their own they need to address and get help with, but we also have roles to play in making sure it doesn't happen again and we handle the situation properly. Many of us sin again, and we tend to repeat the same sin. Just asking for forgiveness isn't enough. Unlike a murderer, the reason why sexual offenders not only do time in jail but have to register themselves as sex offenders is that they are most likely to do it again. Asking for forgiveness and admitting that what you have done is wrong is a good first step. However, we still need to know that there are consequences to our actions.

We also need to shift the attention away from the abuser and go back to abused children. What are we saying to the victim when we give the perpetrator a free pass?

Loving unconditionally does not cancel out the need for setting boundaries. Communicating with our friends and family can be the most stressful and challenging thing to do. We tend to think it's easy because these are supposed to be the people we are closest to, but that's not always the case. Why is communicating with the people closest to us so difficult?

Controversial Topics

Controversial topics cause discomfort, whether it's about a long-existing family feud, politics, or who's house Christmas will be hosted in the following year. When there is a controversial topic, we forget how to listen and feel the need for our point to be heard or to be right. We should instead listen and try to understand someone else's perspective. We fear doing this because accepting another point of view could mean abandoning our own beliefs or views. However, the opposite happens. We gain new insight, and we experience personal growth when we are open to varying perspectives.

Communication Style

Let's be honest, most of us are not very good at communicating. In college, most of us learn about giving presentations but not how to share our viewpoints with loved ones. In kindergarten, we learn how to say please and thank you, but we aren't taught how to communicate with people we disagree with within an informal setting that is not monitored. When are we supposed to learn all of this stuff? The answer is from our family members, but as a teacher and fellow human being, I can tell you most of us don't learn this or only learn much about communication from family.

We all communicate differently. There are also different communication styles depending on cultural background, a person's age, the relationship, and family unit. For some of us, being open about our feelings comes easily, while others struggle and choose to keep their thoughts and feelings to themselves instead.

Then there is the manner of sharing those views and opinions. Some of us are loud and outspoken; others are quiet and soft-spoken. Still others are passionate or animated when they communicate. Our tone, body language and facial expressions also help us express our true feelings.

Another critical aspect of communication that is often misinterpreted is our nonverbal cues and the messages people sometimes give out. "Fix your face," is something my mom would always say to me because, as an animated individual, a look of disagreement or unhappiness always appears on my face before I verbalized my feelings.

Today, most of us are familiar with the term RBF, or the Resting B**** Face. This is the facial expression that makes people think you are a mean person, that you don't care, or for some reason don't like someone. Most of the time, the expression is misinterpreted. The person may be thinking about what they want to eat for lunch or how to get out of a meeting.

If we haven't learned how to communicate properly, then it should be no surprise that miscommunication is the result. When it comes to family, the best way to communicate is to have patience and check your communication style (and be sensitive to theirs) so you can reduce the likelihood of misinterpretation. Also, know which communication style to use and when.

When in doubt, ask questions before you assume what the other person is trying to say, otherwise, you will misinterpret something, and now you are caught assuming the worst of that person. Don't jump to conclusions, especially if you do not know the person, but try to understand their way of thinking. If you do not understand what someone is trying to communicate, you need to stop, ask questions to clarify what they're saying, and refrain from passing judgment. When miscommunication happens, it needs to be addressed right away.

Instead of expressing what you think the other person said, express what you interpreted from their communication. There is a difference between what you hear and what you interpret. If you tell someone they meant to say something other than what they said, once again, you are forcing your views and mindset on them and not seeking to understand them, but telling them to communicate how you communicate based on your lack of understanding. To avoid this, you must have an open mind and assume positive intent, of course, if this is happening consistently, you guys need to talk about it in order to build and maintain a healthy relationship. And it's okay to ask again if you need further clarification on what someone is trying to communicate.

Most of the time, someone misinterprets the message, tone, body language, etc. Ask questions to understand, and don't speak just to respond. Realize that your opinion isn't always helpful, sometimes we just need to be quiet and listen. If you find you are the only one sharing your opinion constantly, there might be a problem. Why is that?

The Need to Win!

Some people like to have the last word and others feel the need to put other people "in their place." In both scenarios, one person is right, and the other is wrong. This mindset is not constructive because, when someone communicates to win, they inevitably push their agenda and perspective onto others. The consequence is typically that the other person will shut down and stop listening altogether. Sometimes people need to debate and, in those instances, right and wrong are more likely to come into play as each person presents their case. In communication with loved ones and family members, however, this form of communication is less likely to be conducive to maintaining a loving familial bond.

Fear of Losing Someone You Love

Don't get me wrong! Sharing your opinion is essential, and there will be times when you will need to make a point that is non-negotiable and not up for discussion. However, it is not likely to happen as often as we think. There are two reasons why this is the case.

Our day-to-day conversations are not likely to present a situation where you need to assert a non- negotiable stance. Your personal life decisions, career choices, parenting style, marital concerns, and finances do not concern anyone besides you, your spouse and/or your kids. Anyone else outside of this group needs to keep their personal opinions (which they might think are valuable) to themselves. There is no place or room for this unless you ask for it.

When this form of communication does need to happen, we may be afraid of damaging our relationships. If you are continually sharing unsolicited advice, you need to be aware of it and stop. Also realize your way isn't always going to be the right way or the preferred way. It may be the best way for you, but not for others.

You are not God and we need to give others the time and space for personal growth, even if your opinion might be helpful. It is not your job to tell other adults how to live their lives, especially when they do not seek out your input. Take a hint: if they have not asked you for your advice, then they probably don't want it, and there is a reason for that. Know you are not the only "all-knowing smart person" in their life, and they probably have others to go to who can offer guidance when they need it. Do not assign the role of correcting others to yourself, but continue developing a relationship with that person. Let others decide if they want your input and focus on maintaining a healthy relationship.

If you are an individual who is receiving unsolicited advice or opinions from others on matters they do not have a say in, you need to address this because they may not stop because they think it's okay. You must set clear boundaries, and this can be difficult because the people who tend to offer unsolicited advice or unwanted opinions tend to be our family. They want the best for you, or maybe they think they know best.

If you're living with your parents, then they have a say. Otherwise, you need to set clear boundaries. While you may worry about hurting your closest relationships, you're only hurting yourself if you don't find a way to respectfully and lovingly say "no, thank you" to unsolicited feedback from loved ones.

The same applies to in-laws. Don't let your marriage suffer because you have failed to set clear boundaries. Know that it is far easier to have a conversation about boundaries before you are married or at the beginning of the marriage so later you only need to remind others if necessary. Although setting boundaries means you are taking control of your life, most families will understand. However, we do not live in a cookie-cutter world, and you need to understand it's not your job to please others nor are you responsible for their happiness at the risk of giving up yours.

The Bible says, "Am I now trying to win the approval of human beings or God? Or am I trying to please people? If I were still trying to please people, I would not be a servant of Christ." (Galatians 1:10 NIV)

The exciting part about this quote is that we tend to apply this to everyone but our family. We must remember that we naturally want to please our family because we are conditioned to from childhood. When we do something our parents like, they may jump up and down and reward us, and it feels good to make them happy. However, that is not our goal, nor our purpose in life, and we have to remind ourselves that, although it may sound harsh, we were not created to get approval nor give happiness to others. You will make mistakes, and your family will disagree with some of your decisions, but if God leads you down a certain path, don't expect them to understand or like it because it is not for them. This can and will be difficult, but to grow as an adult and Christian, you must learn how to fail, succeed, and stand on your own two feet as well as believe in God's purpose for your life.

The best part about unconditional love is coming to terms with the fact that we don't need to strive to please others if we love ourselves unconditionally. We can love those around us without trying to impress them or forcing them to see us a certain way. Loving someone might not always feel like rainbows and kittens, but the consistency and truth that comes from that kind of love will change and positively impact everyone. Unconditional love is not about loving blindly or engaging in unhealthy relationships. It's about maintaining a healthy awareness and balance with those we care about. Not everyone will understand this.

Discussion Questions

1. Do you have healthy boundaries within your existing intimate relationships? (Intimate in this context, meaning close, i.e., family, friends, partners, lovers, etc.) If so, what kind of boundaries?

2. How do you create healthy boundaries with people you are close with?

3. How do/should you monitor your boundaries and hold people accountable, including yourself?

4. When is communicating with people you are closest to challenging? What topics? Why do you think it is difficult to speak about those topics? Try to focus on what you can do differently.

5. Do you find yourself fearing losing someone who is supposed to be close to you and not scared off easily? How can you deepen that relationship?

6. How can you overcome wanting acceptance from others?

7. Is it healthy to want acceptance, and when is it not beneficial?

Here are some useful ideas that have worked for me when feeling the need to be accepted or loved by others.

First, I ask myself what will being accepted by this person do for me? How will it benefit me?

As I'm thinking about these questions, I keep in mind that, although it would be awesome, not everyone in the world will accept me no matter what I do. It is essential to evaluate this relationship to see if it is worth my time and energy.

Second, do I feel pressured to change because if I were my authentic self, it wouldn't work? If the answer is yes, then I need to walk away.

However, if I am trying to change myself for the better, maybe this relationship is worth it.

CHAPTER NINE

AN IMPERFECT LOVE FOR AN IMPERFECT BEING

DO WE TRULY SUPPORT MESSING UP?

There is no such thing as a stupid question.
Lies!
It's okay to mess up, just try.
If you fail, fail forward and it will be all right.
All lies!

Why?
Because people ask stupid questions all the time!
Because just trying isn't enough unless you show
    results after you mess up.
Because if you fail, people don't immediately see your
    potential, but your failure.
Because mistakes breed fear
of the possibility that we can't get better than the now
    and here.

We wish for a world that will support failing and
    messing up,
but laugh and mock those who lose.
We never praise a second or last place.
Never encourage someone depending on their
    mistake.

We don't truly support messing up,
but what we hope comes after it,
and that's victory.
No one worships defeat.
Just as a person who has failed doesn't scream, 'look
    at me!'
It's in triumph that we support.
It's in the before and after,
but not really the before.

And why is that?
Because we have fear that if we celebrate failure
we will become trapped and comfortable with the
    before and never seek the after.

To truly support someone messing up means to know
    how to help.
To know how to be patient and refrain from judgment.
It means understanding that messing up is a
    starting point.
It means to understand that failure does not always
    equate to bad.
And when we finally understand, only then, can we
    move forward as a society instead of back.

An Imperfect Stranger

So, I'm supposed to not only love a stranger but an imperfect stranger? An imperfect stranger is a stranger that you don't even want to get to know. They're flawed, and you don't need to have a deep relationship with them to know this. Immediately my mind goes to murderers, rapists, and the most extreme kinds of imperfect strangers, but some strangers are flawed and are not even that extreme.

I'm prepping my ninth-grade class for a debate a week before it's scheduled. The subject of the debate is, "Can a hero still be a hero if they have messed up?" I use examples like Martin Luther King Jr, a colossal figure in the civil rights movement and highly referred to for his "I Have a Dream" speech and for his messages as a preacher.

"Did you know that MLK, Jr. was also an adulterer?" I ask the class.

My students are speechless for a moment. I watch as they scrunch up their faces in shock and disbelief. "So does knowing this make him less of a hero or cancel out his hero title?" Everyone is quiet.

I then bring up Demi Lovato, who has helped many young people by sharing her story and how she has dealt with bullying and self-confidence issues, but point out how she has lost the battle to drug addiction once again.

"Does her relapse make her less of a good role model or hero?"

The students begin writing in their notebooks. I give them one more example. The example is Lance Armstrong, a professional road racing cyclist and cancer survivor who serves as a beacon of hope for those who suffer from cancer.

"He won many races and medals, but it was later discovered that he was on steroids. He cheated. Is he still a hero?"

My students once again return to their notebooks and record what they feel is the appropriate response to the question.

Fast forward to after work when I'm at home and today's lesson pops up in my head. When I fail, does my failure negate everything positive deed I have done? Does it mean I am no longer worthy of love? I smile to myself because I know God loves me unconditionally and that when I do fail, I will make sure to make things right. But what happens when other people fail? I know I should still show them love, but can I? I think of someone betraying me or hurting me and I conclude that, since I am not God, it's okay if I don't love everyone because at least God will love them, and he can forgive me. If you are an imperfect being, does that mean you only deserve an imperfect love? If we are broken and inconsistent, can we only receive inconsistent and broken love? You get what you deserve. I'm such a hypocrite. If I got what I deserved based upon all my failures, there would be no reason I should be loved. Failure is inevitable but loving someone through their failures is an unavoidable choice we have to make.

Do we genuinely support making mistakes?

We should first clarify what is meant when we refer to mistakes. When you look up what "mistake" means, it will say something along the lines of doing or saying something that is misguided or wrong. The definition is broad; for instance, it doesn't specify what type of action you must do for it to be considered wrong. However, we have placed a hierarchy on specific cases and the type of mistakes that are not okay.

In my first couple years of teaching, I came out of college ready to work and pursue my dreams through hard work. I accepted my first teaching position a couple months after graduating with my master's degree in teaching. I was excited to start my new life as an adult, so much so that, a few months after I accepted my teaching position, I accepted a summer job for teaching and then within a couple more months, a coaching position for track at a different high school then the one I was teaching at. I also accepted to be the advisor for the Black Student Union club and the role of being a youth leader at my church. The following year, I got married and accept another coaching position at a third school to coach basketball.

Not only was I doing all of these different roles but, because I was ashamed at the time and fully believed in my own capabilities, I refused to ask for help because I thought I could handle things. I quickly learned that I had made a mistake. Not only was I overworking myself, but I wasn't getting the help I needed to keep my sanity, and it showed in different parts of my life.

Although my decision was misguided because I believed working hard meant I should do everything I was capable of, I wasn't able to execute as well within my different roles. However, because I was fresh out of college and the mistake I made was very common for people my age and in my profession, I received a little more grace because people could relate to me. Co-workers from my teaching job would tell me, "Dang, you do all that? How are you not tired or burnt out? I remember when I was your age and I did the same thing. Try not to overwork yourself."

So, when we ask if we truly support making mistakes, I believe it depends on the mistake. It depends on the person's age, sex, race, ethnicity, sexual orientation, and religion before society judges whether we support the error. We judge our fellow humans' mistakes based upon these different categories and determine if we truly support their mistake.

When people are young, we expect them to make mistakes and fail more often that is the norm. However, we have also linked making mistakes with having a problem. For example, if you make a mistake, it might be because you did not practice enough, you weren't following instructions, or you did something harmful to cause the mistake. Because of this mindset, we have more young people afraid of making mistakes because they fear to confirm those negative connotations attached to it and we automatically assume our mistake equals failure when that is not always the case.

The language we use when communicating with young people can lead to creating a negative impact when we don't consider the negative connotations the words we use have. For example, we may use statements like, "It's probably because they're so young." "She only said that because she must be confused." "I don't think they understand." Americans also use these exact phrases to describe people they might think may be incompetent or disagreeable. No-one wants to feel like they don't fit in, which is why young people today strive so much to avoid failure.

While we encourage students to make mistakes because they can always get to the correct answer and succeed afterward, that's the root of the problem around mistakes. As a society, we don't support mistakes. Why do you think we get so frustrated when our kids constantly struggle to solve a math problem?

Once we're frustrated enough, we just give them the answer. Why? Because we don't truly support making mistakes.

Making mistakes multiple times

Now let us get into the amount. Even if making a mistake is something as simple as a little white lie, you can only do that so many times before people question what is wrong with you, your intentions, and then proceed to label you. The problem with this is that, instead of assessing the entire situation, we jump to labeling and indicating what we assume to be the problem: you. This is a problem because we never once considered the reasoning and intent in the situation, which also plays a part. What if the reason for someone's little white lie is to avoid hurting another's feelings? If the intentions are good, does that excuse the mistake?

The danger of making the same mistake multiple times is, after lying multiple times, it can become a habit rather than a mistake and then we find ourselves lying for everything and anything just because we are used to it. The intention can start off as meaning well but can help feed into your negative habit. For a mistake to be considered a mistake, we resort back to the dog-eat-dog world, and if you can't become better after a mistake, then that is a problem. The question then is: What is the number of times you can make mistakes before it is no longer considered a mistake?

This is hard because, as Christians, we know that we sin repeatedly, but God isn't sitting over our shoulder saying, "Okay, that was the last mistake, and now you are going to hell." We are trying to be "like" Jesus, but we are not him, so we struggle to offer grace and forgiveness. The real question then becomes if a person makes a mistake or messes up repeatedly and never learns from their mistake, it is no longer a mistake, it is intentional, correct?

If we revisit our example about lying and how intentions can impact that, then we see the importance of it. When you tell a white lie for the first time, we are not intentionally trying to lie, but the intent is to make someone feel good. For example, if I were to tell a little white lie about how someone looks, my intent is to make them feel good, but my mistake is that they are asking me for the truth so that they can choose what to wear and I did not give them accurate information. After learning I made a mistake in my assuming they could not handle the truth, if I continue to lie knowing I have made a mistake, I am now intentionally lying and so it is no longer a mistake, it is a habit. Intentionally acting or saying something we know is not right is not a mistake.

Backgrounds have limits

There is inequality between races, where people of color are often given fewer opportunities to mess up before they are reprimanded harshly or killed. In contrast, white people are not, and we see that with issues, such as police brutality. The reason for this tends to be based on stereotypes. If a person of color makes a mistake, they are inherently evil, thugs or hoodlums, and it was their INTENTION to do so. If a white person makes a mistake, it must be a genuine mistake and was not actually their intention, and if it was, then it is because they have mental health issues and need to be handled "gently." People of color aren't given the "mental health" issues option, but that is another topic.

A person's age is also an indicator of how many mistakes they can make and what those mistakes can be. A small example would be that if a child hit an adult with the intent to play, they get a pass because we assume they are still learning. But if a teenager were to hit another adult or teen, we would not only question what is wrong with them, but we would then go as far to label them as aggressive.

When children make mistakes, we understand it's because they are still learning, but then we assume that once they reach adulthood, they will have learned all the cultural norms of being an adult. However, what are those norms, and is there a list we can all access? Who is responsible for teaching those norms? Teachers? Parents? The community? By what age should we all know those norms?

As I think about all of these questions, I can't help but ask what exactly what does loving unconditionally mean? If people suck, how can we love them unconditionally? I believe it means no one has to pay us back for our love, but it is safe and okay for us to set healthy boundaries and to take care of ourselves. When thinking of someone who messes up, it can be easy for our minds to go to the worst-case scenarios in which loving an individual like this can be challenging; however, if we do, we should do so without expecting anything in return. It is difficult because, someone who repeatedly makes mistakes without growth or change is no longer making mistakes. However, everyone learns and changes at different speeds and, again, I should not expect anything in return for loving someone.

Failure as an endpoint vs. a new beginning

Finally, when it comes to messing up and whether we support people making mistakes or not, we tend to associate errors with failure. If you mess up, you have automatically failed in many people's minds. However, the problem is not with the mistake itself but with the notion that we see failure as an endpoint instead of a launching pad into a new beginning. Seeing others' failures as a chance for a fresh start can help us understand that one, we are not called to judge, and two, everyone has the potential to change.

Will Smith said that if you are going to fail, then fail forward. There is nothing wrong with failure unless you allow yourself to remain in that space of failure. After that, you need to keep moving forward. The lack of moving forward or growing is what we have a problem with. Failure is not an endpoint but should rather be seen as a fresh start; a new beginning to learn from what has happened in the past and to start a new quest to a better future. It is a second chance.

With failure must come growth; without growth, it's easy to walk away. However, this is a sign to make sure we are setting healthy boundaries. We can still love others while taking care of ourselves. I can't count the number of times I failed or bothered my parents, siblings, or husband. There have been times where I have been ungrateful and acted like a spoiled brat, yet they love me unconditionally. I believe it is easier for that to happen because they see growth. But what happens when someone constantly makes mistakes, and there is no change. Should we still love them?

"He's at it again," my friend Judy whispers under her breath. She is three inches shorter than me with an athletic build and curly hair. A lot of people mistake us for sisters even though she is a little lighter than me.

It was fall and my friends and I were walking on the sidewalk on our way to my house. I watch as a shell of a man walks up to us. He wore a dingy black puffer coat with rags for shirts and dirty baggy jeans. He smiles at her with most of his teeth missing. The rest of us exchange confused looks because we have no clue who this man is. They talk for a few minutes, and I can see it hurts her just to speak with him.

"Well, I'm glad you are doing better." She swallows and forces a smile.

"Yeah, I just need a couple of dollars to cover this month's rent since I got a new place. You know it's hard with everything going on and getting out of rehab and stuff, just trying to stay afloat right now."

I don't believe a word he says, and we all know why. I want to try and bail her out and tell her we have to go, but she responds before I can move.

"Oh really, how much is a couple of dollars?" "It's not much, like five hundred dollars or so."

He shrugs and looks around before looking back at her almost to check if he gave a reasonable price. My eyes go wide at what he believes to be a "couple of dollars."

"Okay, we can talk about that later. I haven't seen you in a while, so let's catch up for a bit."

They walk away, but not for long. When she comes back, she has a fake smile plastered on her face, and the guy she was with is walking in the opposite direction of us.

"We can go" she doesn't even manage to hold a smile before crying. We all hug her and let her know it will be okay even though we don't understand everything. Once we get to my place, she spills her guts. We are in my bedroom sitting in a little circle on the floor with nothing but my desk light on and the door cracked, letting the hallway light sneak in.

She tells us about the addiction, the broken promises, the cycles, and the consistency of her brother's inconsistency. She tells us all of this, and in my head, I can't help but wonder a few things. First, how can she forgive him? I understand that he is her brother and that a familial bond is not broken so easily, but when someone is so unhealthy and toxic, how can you love them unconditionally? Grace. She wipes her tears away.

"I know there is good in him still. Even now, I know he is fighting to get his life back. Even though it might not look like it."

I don't believe it is forgiveness of his failures that has kept her love burning for her brother, but her hope and desire for better.

"I pray he will no longer have to endure the temptation but will overcome this." I tell her. She inhales deeply as if taking it all in before speaking.

"Thank you," she breathes, "Okay, enough about my family stuff let's play *Uno*." We all laugh and do a big group hug before I scramble to grab the *Uno* cards from under my bed. The rest of the night continues with chill conversation, a little bit of gossip and lots of *Uno* before everyone heads home. Before we know it, hours have passed and we are saying our goodbyes.

"Bye guys, thanks for coming over!" I open the front door for them.

"Bye!" They both say before giving me another hug.

"We have to do this again," Judy says, "And thank you for listening to me," she whispers before running down to her parent's car and waving goodbye once more. I wait until I can no longer see their cars before I close the door and head to my room. I'm alone in my room, and I can't shake this feeling of uncertainty. Giving grace when I feel grace is undeserved, loving when I can't find something to love, and forgiving when the pain exceeds what I want to overlook is far more complicated than I realize. I think of my friend's situation, and I realize the first thing I struggle with is dealing with someone who is unhealthy, and their failure impacts me directly. Can I love them while maintaining my health and sanity? Of course, I can. There is no rule or healthy individual in this world that will tell you to sacrifice your mental state to love unhealthy people. Loving from a distance is real. I can support my loved ones without supporting their addictions or unhealthy habits. Like my friends, I can love someone because I know who they can be and the beauty inside them without loving or supporting their actions or negative habits.

It might look like just having a conversation and checking in, praying for them even when they don't know it. Showing grace and forgiving frees *me* of any bondage and allows God to take over any situation I was already unqualified to take care of. Loving this imperfect being is not just important because they need it, but because loving them also impacts everyone they touch.

As I'm thinking of all of this, I think of my own life and what I experienced as a kid, and how I could move on from what happened. I still feel disgusted after it all. How do I love and show grace? I squirm in my bed and try not to think of everything from my past. Can there be good in someone who does something like that? I want nothing to do with him. Never to see him again or encounter his presence. I hope the best for him and that he can grow so that something like this never happens to anyone else again. Is that love? Am I showing grace?

After thinking about all of this, I get angry. Why do I have to show grace? Why am I the one thinking of how to love this person unconditionally? When I was the victim, I was hurt, and

I am the child?! I throw my pillow across the room as my chest tightens. I take a strained breath before exhaling and flopping back on my bed. What difference does it make? I'll never see him again. I bring my blanket to my face and doze off for what I think is a few seconds, but when I wake up, it's morning. I rub my crusty eyes before walking to my window and peering outside. On a new day, I pray he has changed and continues to change. I wish him the best. I don't think I can physically use the word *love* with him. Thinking of it makes me cringe, but I believe that this is good enough and all I can do right now. I will never support what he did or his negative actions, but the opportunity and chance for him to change is something I hope for and can get behind.

Discussion Questions

1. How often do you make mistakes? When do you feel like you have failed? At what point do you feel like you can no longer afford to make a mistake?

2. How many times do you believe someone can make a mistake? If someone can mess up repeatedly, what is the appropriate response as a Christian? Can you still distance yourself and ensure you are healthy while offering someone grace or forgiveness?

3. At what point do we make other people's mistakes about ourselves? When and why do we enter ourselves into the equation of other people's mess-ups? What are the dangers of doing this? How can we prevent it?

4. Do you support messing up? What does that support look like if you do? What about your inner circle? Do they support you messing up? Does your family or spouse?

5. What does messing up look like within a family, marriage, workspace, parent-child relationship? What does support for it look like?

CHAPTER TEN

HELP ROOTED IN LOVE

HELP

The truth about helping is
we don't know how to help.
In fact,
often when we do help
we are actually hurting.

We don't have the patience to truly allow someone
   to grow,
so in our efforts to help
we take over and do it for them,
stunting potential growth or making it slow.

We assume our presence and help is far more
   important.
Or that our help and feedback is the one needed.
We assume whatever we give is best because
we believe it.

We never ask what the need is,
but post it on social media
to be glorified.
Like look at this poor kid,
I gave him shoes.
But pain and poverty isn't something people choose.
So why does their life become our promotion?
Their personal story is stripped and altered so people
can understand our devotion.

Ima' say this one time and one time only.

Help in silence.

Don't look for a reward.
I get it!
You want to promote your new program or business
but people's trials and tribulations aren't meant
for your extortion or a promotion.
It's not so you can convince the world how you are a
good person.

True help is difficult,
because you have to watch people struggle,
and do your best to provide them with what they need,
while maintaining distance so they can succeed.

True help is difficult,
because as the helper

we have our own motivation and intention for why we
   are helping,
which in some cases can create
a detrimental impact.

You see, we don't understand helping
because helping is necessary
but receiving something in return is not.
True help doesn't have a cost.

IN NEED OF A HAND

We are stuck in a time where we say here are my
    problems
world, figure out a way to deal with me
because I don't know how to deal with myself.
I have anxiety, and trauma.
However, we all have anxiety and trauma,
so, shifting the responsibility to heal your anxiety
and trauma when I'm still learning to heal
and deal with my own isn't going to help
because at the end of the day
when you go home,
it's going to be you,
your trauma,
and your anxiety.

So, when you say
I have anxiety and trauma,
are you trying to say,
what has worked for you, so that
maybe it will work for me too?

Or are you trying to say,
I have these problems,
and that should be counted as an adequate excuse
as to why I was...
a. inappropriate,
b. not putting in effort or
c. rude
'cause there is a difference.

178

HELP ROOTED IN LOVE

What is your specific need?
Someone to listen to your problems?
Someone to show empathy and not sympathy?
Someone to give advice?
Someone to turn a blind eye?

We have conditioned each other into thinking help
means providing the answer or solution,
so when we ask for help
we aren't really asking for help,
but for someone to solve our problems.
To do the work for us,
as many have done in the past.

We are conditioning our kids to be forever
dependent
and then we get mad when they fail,
or decide to come back
because they can't make decisions for themselves.

The truth about helping is,
we need to first help ourselves
before we can help anyone else,
and then understand that
helping is not providing the answers,
but acting as a guide,
so that others can get to them.

When Helping Hurts

When I was younger, I went to Mexico on two separate occasions to do mission trips with my mom. Then, as I got older, I was able to join my mom and the rest of my family on a mission trip to Africa.

It's the summer of our trip to Africa. I just graduated from college and am dating Kalen. My parents bring my siblings and I into the hospitality area of the church so we can continue training on why we are doing this mission trip and reviewing some safe traveling tips.

"We are going to Uganda and Rwanda as the first stop of many mission trips to come," My mom explains.

"This first trip is for us to go and see what they need or want from us so that, when we return, we can provide exactly what they asked for."

We all shake our heads, waiting for more because my parents have been traveling and doing mission trips for a while, so we are very familiar with the protocol, even if this is our very first trip all together as a family.

"We don't want to assume anything, especially as outsiders," My dad says. "They are not incapable, nor do they need us."

"Exactly," my mom interrupts, "As servants, for us to serve, we need to know what it is we should serve and what is the best way to serve it. We are to merely be used as the hands and feet of God and nothing else."

Next, they explain the rest of the training and safety protocol such as stay together as a group when traveling and where we should put our passport. Finally, we all leave the meeting amped up and ready to go on the trip.

Time flies by, and before we know it, it is time to leave. After twenty-one hours of flying, we finally arrived in Uganda. The earth is a beautiful shade of red and radiates natural warmth. The people we walk by have an air of confidence and an elegance I can't quite put into words.

When we arrive at the house we will be staying in, we unload our luggage. Immediately, my mom lets us know we have a meeting with the leaders. We go outside and I can't help but be excited to be in the presence of the others. We all take turns introducing ourselves, what we do, how old we are, and why we are excited to be here in Uganda.

The leaders have been carefully listening to everything we say. They ask us what we think about Uganda and what we look forward to doing during the process? My siblings and I explain how we are excited to learn and absorb anything and everything while also sharing whatever we can that they might want to know. One of the leaders smiles and explains how they have worked with different missionaries and mission groups before and have had not-so-great experiences where the mission group thinks they are going to come into Uganda and save them.

"They come already with a plan, and yet they have never once asked what it is that we need or what we can use that will be something we can sustain? They come with this idea that they are here to save us, and that Africa is just this ugly and terrible place, but as you can see, Africa is beautiful, and we do not need saving," one of the leaders explains.

I completely agree, and so does the rest of my family. As my parents and the leaders begin to talk about logistics and a plan for future visits now that we all understand and are on the same page, my mind drifts back to a class I took in college. We looked at mission trips and how there are ample amounts of opportunities where helping can hurt people instead of help them. In the class, we addressed how easy it is to adopt a savior mentality and put ourselves on pedestals. I remember one of my classmates making a comment.

"But what if the person we are helping puts us on a pedestal? What then?" The teacher doesn't hear her, as the comment was never meant for the teacher's ears, but I do.

"Then you just take yourself off," I said. She looked at me, surprised.

"If we are doing a mission trip, we can easily mistake another's cultural practices as worship because their hospitality might be better than that of the United States', and they are not actually putting us on a pedestal but just showing us love. However, we can always redirect worship and properly direct it to God."

"That's so true. I never thought about it that way," she begins taking notes. I tell her I can't take credit because I learned this myself from my parents.

I end my reflection and bring my thoughts back to Uganda in the circle of leaders. The meeting ends, and I'm walking to the room my siblings and I will be sharing.

I reflect on the question the leaders asked us, "What are you looking forward to doing while in Uganda?" I'm not here to save anyone nor tell anyone how to live. I am here because

I want to show love, and I don't expect anything back, no praise, thank you, money, or for them to come to America and help my family when we might need help. I realize I don't know how we will help yet, but I hope I can just listen to what they want to happen and come with an open mind.

If I am to help in any way, I want to make sure my help is rooted in unconditional love. I am open to offering whatever support they might need. At least, this is the mindset I have in that moment, but when we get to Misaka, and the school leaders ask us for a basketball court, my mind immediately imagines the best outside basketball court in Oregon.

Oooh, it would be tight, especially with the red earth, to get a dope red basketball court like the one at our neighborhood park and glass backboards! They would love it. After seeing what they were playing on for a basketball court, I wanted them to experience what I experienced at home, but it was with this thinking that I made a big mistake. I assumed they liked my experience and that my experience was the best option for them. Luckily, I only voiced my idea to my parents before my parents explained we would need to build a court with materials they can't find here in Africa. Nor could they afford to maintain it themselves and not depend on us to manage it from America. I nod my head and realize I still have a lot of room for personal growth.

The Truth About Helping

As a teacher, I've learned the most crucial part of teaching and helping students is knowing when to just shut up. We talk too much. Whether you are a boss, parent, administrator, teacher, mentor, etc., it is likely no-one wants to listen and learn from your direct instruction. Please stop trying to solve other people's problems for them. This does not help; it only hurts them in the long run. Just stop talking!

If you don't believe me, go to therapy or counseling session. When you seek help from a therapist or counselor, their job is to help you — not to tell you what to do. They listen patiently to you and guide you on what you already know and remind about what you already believe. In other words, you walk in, and you do all the talking while they listen. Of course, they might have something to add here and there, but they allow you to come to the answers on your own and in your own time. Your experiences with success and failure are what will help you figure out what works.

If our help is rooted in love, our focus isn't on how the results will impact us but how it will transform the person we're attempting to help.

When I wanted the Misaka basketball court to look precisely like the basketball court I had played on in my neighborhood, I wanted to see how the students would like it. I wanted them to experience something the way I did. However, the focus was on me and what I would receive in the end, which was the reaction and satisfaction of making them be more like me.

Why do we make helping others about ourselves? Helping takes time, and it's not always an enjoyable process. It can be tedious. As teachers, spouses, family members, and bosses, we want to hurry up and get to the end result. The fastest way to do this is to provide the answers only when it seems our students don't understand, or our partner is taking too long to get the idea, or our kids just keep doing the opposite of what we ask them to. Why do you think most people hate group projects? It's because help that is rooted in unconditional love is challenging and time- consuming. It's a lot easier to just do the whole project by ourselves, or so we think.

By providing answers instead of guidance, we also take away another person's opportunity to experience whatever the consequences may be. So, whether the result is harmful because you were right all along and of course they shouldn't have touched a burning stove after you told them not to, or they are optimistic because times have changed, or they just operate differently than you do so they don't have to study to get an A, they still learn by what works for them.

The truth about helping is we don't want to help people, but we want to make them into a copy of ourselves. We don't know the answers to life, but we know what has worked for us, and we get our way confused with "the way" that can work for everyone else. What worked for us might not work for everyone. Listen before you speak, and sometimes, don't speak at all.

Oh, unsolicited advice

We think we know more than we do. The difficulty of helping is knowing when your help is needed and when it is not. Sometimes we think highly of ourselves, especially if we are in leadership roles. For example, as teachers, sometimes we forget that, yes, we may know more about how to write a paper in the MLA format than our fourteen-year-olds but that does not make us superior to them or all-knowing. There are definitely some things those fourteen-year-olds know that we don't.

As adults, it's easy to look at a younger person and assume we know what's best based upon our own experience. However, each generation is different, and no two individuals are the same. While there is much to learn from older generations, I do not think copy and paste solutions can be effective. It can be humbling to think that experience alone may not equip us well enough to effectively guide a younger generation. Admitting we do not know everything can feel uncomfortable, but we have to come to terms with the fact that we may not have all the answers.

It's like when you have been taught to keep your room clean and it's currently very messy. After school today, you decide you will clean your room after you do your homework. However, when you get home, and you're about to start cleaning, your mom or dad says, "Make sure you clean that room!" then instantly all your motivation is lost. Why is that? Because one of your parents took away the momentum you needed to make your own decisions. And because your parent's request can mean:

1. They don't trust you or believe you are responsible enough to remember to clean your room

2. They feel you need to hear them say it because you haven't done it on your own initiative.

This may be a simple example, but it applies to other areas of our lives. Often, we take away an individual's chance to be independent by interfering when they finally get the momentum to act on their own.

Can we just help?

I've found, especially during times of crisis, that we make helping others more difficult than it needs to be. We want so badly to be recognized that we forget why we are helping in the first place. We would let someone starve Monday through Thursday so that we could be the ones to shake their hand on Friday. We want credit for being the ones who provided for them. This approach can only rip away the pride and dignity of a struggling parent whose children bear witness to the fact that their parents cannot provide for themselves. Why can't we give while remaining anonymous?

Why do we exploit helping situations and opportunities for our benefit? We do this because our intentions aren't to help others but to develop a program, an initiative, and a business or to talk about ourselves and to be recognized for what we do and what we give. Our intention is not to truly help people. I say this because if we intended to truly help people, then we would take out the recognition part, and the politics. We would just offer to assist, which would also allow us to help far more people.

There is a difference between marketing your services and marketing all the details of how you serviced a specific family or individual without their permission. If and when we help, it should be based and rooted in unconditional love and not painting a positive image of ourselves or our personal branding.

When we share how we help, especially on social media, we should ask ourselves what the purpose is. What does the image say we are sharing? Does it paint a savior mentality story? Or does it support your excitement to serve others? I think these questions are helpful to keep in mind when posting or sharing what you might do as a helper.

Before you help someone, you can also take time to reflect on the answers to these questions.

"Why do I want to help?"

"Am I expecting something in return?"

"What do I expect in return?"

Know that you can begin the process of helping in a way that is rooted in unconditional love. It's important to check in with yourself along the way. Recognize what your end goal is while making sure the person or group you are engaging with understands what this relationship is supposed to look like and what to expect. As I have stated countless times in this book, communication is key to avoiding hurting someone when you are actually intending to help.

Asking for & Receiving help

How do we ask for help in a country that tells us to pull ourselves up by our own bootstraps while fighting against a system that was not created to benefit every human being? In moments like this, we have to love ourselves unconditionally to understand that asking for help is not a weakness but sometimes a necessity. The simplest way to ask for help, of course, is just to ask. However, it is not that simple due to a few reasons:

1. Pride/ego:

    It can be uncomfortable. Often people assume you are just asking for a handout because, sadly, there are people who take advantage of situations and the systems in place to help people in need.

2. You do not know who to ask.

    This can be difficult because if you ask the wrong people, they might be the ones assuming you are lazy and just want a handout, or they might hold it over your head years later and want you to be forever indebted to them. Lastly, they might attempt to post you in a light that portrays you as a helpless person who needed to be saved by them, which is very unhealthy and disrespectful. They also might not have the resources or network to help you with what you need.

3. You do not know what to ask for.

    A lot of the time, we don't know what we need, but we know we need help. For example, a single mom who knows she needs to pay the bills, feed her children, get new clothes, and maybe even fix her car. The challenging thing about asking for help is we fear asking for money the most because, again, there are people in the world who have broken the trust by exploiting others and using money meant for help/aid on other items. This creates a situation where we're forcing others to struggle through impossible circumstances we may not even know how to relate to. How can we ask a mom to choose between feeding her children and keeping a roof over their heads? What if they do not have family or the support system we assume most people have?

Like anything, we can become accustomed to receiving help. When we are used to someone providing something for us for free or making connections for us, we can depend on that and take advantage of it, which is why, we as helpers need to realize the kind of help required for the given situation. It's always easy to accept the kind of help where the helper does the majority of the work so that we do not have to exert any energy, and although there is a time and place for that type of help, it can be detrimental.

Does genuine help cost anything?

I believe there are different ways to help someone.

1. Pure Help: When you're helping someone out of the goodness of your heart.

2. Emergency Relief or Crisis Response: When someone needs or requests your help because of an urgent situation.

3. Initiative Response: When you help people for personal gain. You may genuinely want to help people and even feel fulfilled by the help you offer, but you, your business, or program is gaining from that help in some way.

Number three is tricky because specific jobs/occupations fall under this category. For example, doctors, teachers, therapists, and so on seek to help people whatever the cost. But, of course, they do these jobs 24/7 and need compensation to live if we wish for them to continue doing what they do. But then this brings us back to the question, what type of help is needed and what kind of help is wanted? Is there a difference, and is there a particular form of assistance that every person can live without?

Does our society honestly know what help is? Most of the time, we believe we are doing the first or second form of helping, but we are actually doing the third. In some cases, we even start at the first or second and somehow wind up at the third.

Is this always true? No. Of course not. There is a time and a place for everything and for every kind of help. However, the question is when? When is each form of help appropriate? When should helping cost something? Should it cost something? What do we mean when we say there is a price for our help or helping costs? Are we talking money, time, energy? What exactly?

Before I end this chapter, I want to dive into what receiving too much help can turn us into. Not only do we become dependent upon that help, but it becomes a part of our identity. We start to seek out the tangible help people might give us but the emotional aspect of that help as well. When someone helps us out of the kindness of their heart, several things happen.

First, we feel as though someone has cast a spotlight on us, and we feel seen. And for some of us, to stay seen, we believe we must always be in a place of need or lack. Pain and despair become our constant dwelling place as we seek to convince those around us that we truly need their help, but we want the attention it brings as it helps us gain some of the things we want.

Most of the time, we don't even realize we desire this attention because our fundamental need for help does start from a place of genuine need or lack. However, sometimes if we are in that space for too long, we can trap ourselves into a situation that keeps us asking for more. Craving this form of help and wrapping it into our identity can lead to an extreme situation where we don't even want to free ourselves from the situation we're in. We have the key to freedom, but we don't want to use it. Help can be misused and abused both by the helper and the person being helped, which is why we first need to understand what real help is before we just dive in and offer or accept it.

Regardless of the form of help we are engaged in; we need to make sure we begin and end the help we give with love. Unconditional love can help keep us centered, even if our help is an initiative or part of our business. It is essential to remind ourselves that most business initiatives or non-profits are started out of the desire to help. Staying rooted in unconditional love can ensure we offer help in the best way possible. We must help with not just our intentions, but with the action that comes with loving unconditionally.

Discussion Questions

1. What is your reason for helping? Is your answer as simple as you just want to help, or is there another reason? If so, why?

2. Can having another reason for helping others be okay? When is it okay if you said yes?

3. Do you find yourself depending more on others for help even though you can do it yourself? When do you do this, and why?

4. Is there a specific situation where it is not okay to receive help? If so, what type of situation? If not, why?

5. How can we identify if we have become too reliant upon the help of others? What are the steps to take if we notice someone near us has become too dependent?

CHAPTER ELEVEN

CHANGE

CHANGE

Do you really want change?
'cause it seems like all we want to know is,
whose holocaust was worse?
Not acknowledging, we both experienced hurt.

We're steady comparing who had more pain
'cause all we care about is who is the true race,
who is superior and,
who is inferior and
no-one wants to be on the bottom,
so we make sure we drag our brothers and sisters
    beneath us
so we can take that one step up.

We consider their failure our victory,
and it's like we forgot all about equality,
it's a mystery.
And now we define who our brothers and sisters are

by the color of their skin.
Instead of the love of God that lies within.

So here I am worrying,
can we ever pick ourselves up
from this world we created for ourselves or are
   we stuck?
And I say, we
because We played a part in creating our world today.

Waiting but not attempting change.
Is it just me?
I mean call me insane
but I feel like all we do today
is complain,
and all I have to say is one simple
question for you,
I feel like the answer is obvious,
but no-one wants to take the responsibility of stepping
   up to the plate.
And all I want to know is...
Do you truly want change?
Or are you content with living in your current ways?
Or are you that person who likes to shift the blame?
You like to state what are you doing to enforce
   change....
I start by making a difference in someone's life one
   step at a time.
I pray every day that God would minimize the crime.

CHANGE

I try to speak life to those who feel like they are dying.
I sit up listening to phone calls of people crying.
I try to be a big sister to someone who is ten years
   older than me.
I reach out to people through poetry.

That's just a little bit of my change,
and you wanna know the difference between you
   and me?
I don't just move my mouth,
I move my feet.
And if you don't even understand that
then don't even bother listening to me.
And I'm saying this because this conversation is all too
   familiar
we get hyped,
excited, motivated,
gain courage on how we gonna change the world,
then when reality hits we get discouraged
and we back down,
and start to complain,
but in our heads we're thinking this isn't sane.
And that speech we give just blows in the wind
until the next motivation speaker comes in,
and then restart all over again.

I stand before you wondering,
Do you? Do you want change?
I'm not asking you to pump your fist.

Or get a million followers,
or feed everyone bread and fish.
I'm just asking for you to make a difference.
Do something!
No fake performing.
Just one thing,
Do you really want change?

This isn't about how to compare and contrast.
It's time for you to get off your rear end
and stand up for what you believe in.
Stop over-thinking things because
it's the little things that matter.
Do what you were meant to do!
Be the best you can be, everyone leads differently.
You can't compare whose change was bigger,
whose impact was greater.
Because in the end,
you will never know.

And change is change
so my question to you is...
Do you really want change?

Change

In my senior year of high school, I received the Act Six scholarship. The scholarship is a full need/full-tuition leadership scholarship to a four-year college. As a requirement, I would have to attend weekly training with my cadre, the other students who also received the scholarship, before we officially attend one of the two universities offered. During these training sessions, while learning about how to combat injustice and protect myself, I began to question how badly I wanted to change the world?

The idea of attending a university where everyone looks different from my fellow cadre members and me, and where we are guaranteed to endure passive-aggressive racism, or blatant racism, did not sound appealing. At eighteen, I'm contemplating why I want to bother changing and if it's even worth it? I truly want everyone to be happy and live a long and prosperous life, but the end result of that desire is not my concern; only the process is. Will I maintain such a positive mindset and outlook on change during the process when I encounter adversity, a multitude of "isms," and constant discouragement? Can I honestly love each individual despite what they might throw at me? Can I turn the other cheek? I'm at a loss for words.

After spacing out during the meeting, I went home that night, and scrolled through social media. Although re-writing history and combating injustice wasn't as popular as it is now, I still found posts highlighting all the work we had to do, which made me ask myself, was all of this worth it? How bad did

I want to change? To what extent? Most importantly, did I want to change? Does the world want to change? Am I going to be fighting a battle where the system in place pretends to be on my side at times, but would rather everything stay the same? Is change just a status quo or a way to save face? Who wants change and why? Why put yourself through so much for only the possibility and not the guarantee of change?

Lost in a sea of questions, I write the poem above and then read it to my cadre. We debriefed and realized now was not a time to give up because what was ahead of us would be tough or daunting. It was not a time to compare our pain, trauma, and people's persecutions. It was time to stand together to heal and fight for what matters to us all, change for the betterment of our future.

It's 2021, and as I had my doubts about change when I was younger. By now, I have answered some of the questions and I learned from experience that, just because the going gets tough it doesn't mean we should give up. In a world where Black Lives Matter seems to be a mixture of a trend and the status quo, I want change more than ever. I realize, too, how battered we are as a nation and human race. But we are not broken, and therefore I will continue to push and fight for change, not just my brothers and sisters, but for my son's future and his sons' and daughters' future. I'm not going to lie that social media has indeed made it difficult at times to have hope or has made me question if this is what I want to do, but I keep coming back to the purpose God has created for me. To answer the question, yes, I want, no, I *need*, change so that everyone, including those who don't yet recognize they need change, can live a better and healthier life.

Love and Gang violence

You can say I'm obsessed. I have dreamt, written poetry, sung songs, danced, and screamed all my life about the need for change. It's practically what I breathe. Throughout my life, I've found that change can be painful but necessary, and that sometimes it can make you beg and plead with God to please fix it overnight. It can even make you question if the change is something the world wants or is just silly to believes we should have it?

One consistent truth remains, and that is that change is necessary. If my life could have a movie title, it might be called the *Pursuit of Change* instead of happiness, or the *Pursuit of Happiness Through Change*. My pursuit of change began at a young age. As a child, my parents taught me to love my neighbors and to turn the other cheek. However, as I found out more about the world and all of the injustice and inequality, I realized I wanted to change our world. I wanted equality for women and minorities. I wanted drug and alcohol abuse to stop, along with all physical abuse. I had high hopes that everything would change quickly, but when gang violence was getting to an all-time high in Portland, my family received some terrible news.

I was finishing my sophomore year in high school when the news came about Billy. I was upstairs when I heard my mom talking with my dad in the kitchen.

"Oh God," she covered her mouth and stared at the phone.

"What?!" my dad asked.

"Billy's dead. He's been shot and killed." "Wasn't he just visiting his mom?!"

"Yeah, they just took her off of life support, and he was getting off of the bus when someone shot him," she covered her mouth again and leaned back into the kitchen cabinets.

"Oh my God," my dad muttered in disbelief.

I was watching and listening from the bottom of the stairs and ran into my room and put my head into my pillow—another life is taken for no good reason. Tears streamed down my cheeks and soaked the dingy pillow I was lying on. "God, please," I sobbed. "Please, just make it stop, no more hurt, no more pain! Just please," I was sobbing so hard my bed was shaking. By the time I finished, I was fast asleep. When I woke up, I grabbed a pen and paper and wrote the poem "Simple Request."

I performed the poem in many places and in front of different audiences. With each performance my intent and desired outcome were the same:

1. I want my words to invoke a change or stir something within the people I am communicating with so that they can spread the word and begin to look at each other differently and treat others differently.

2. I want my words to prove to every young person they are loved and don't need someone else's validation, especially validation or love from an unhealthy group

of people. I want them to realize they are already loved unconditionally. I want them to feel that I love their very existence not because of how they look or what they might do but because they exist.

3. I want to love the victims so they know they are not alone and can connect with other victims and come to understand why they don't need to turn to violence.

4. I want to learn from the perpetrator so they too understand that there is no reason for meaningless violence. And that they should decide not to take others' lives or influence others to behave like them.

I know it's far-fetched idealism, but if I am to pursue change, it has to be rooted in love and people understanding that change begins with them.

Where to start amidst the chaos

Toward the end of my sophomore year in college, I was asked to write a poem to open the TEDx Portland event. The opportunity came from someone I met through a Nike event I performed at earlier. The opportunity with Nike came from a staff member from my high school who had a connection with the company and convinced me to try out for a spoken word commercial.

The day of the audition, I decided to go with my mom. There were young women stretching in the hall and some were doing splits I assumed were related to some choreographed dance moves they likely submitted before the competition. Then there was me. I was sitting on the cold cement floor with my back against the wall, and my knees pulled up to my chest. I was not dressed like a dancer and I definitely didn't fit in.

As soon as my audition was over, the judges were excited and chose me on the spot. It would have been my first international commercial and for Nike at that! However, weeks later, I received a call that although I did well at the audition and I was the one they had originally chosen, I did not have an African accent. That being what they wanted for the commercial, meant they were going to go with someone else. Although I was bummed out, at least Nike now had my contact information and knew what I could do.

I did get called back a few more times to perform poetry at Nike events. The TEDx Portland opportunity came from one of Nike's people.

"Oh my gosh, guess what?!" I exclaimed to my mom.

"What?" She asked unenthusiastically.

"Mom, you have to guess," I say and roll my eyes. "Ummm, you're going to nationals," she says without trying

"No, mom. I just got asked to open TEDx Portland event with a poem on the theme of 'What If?'"

"What?" She screams in excitement more than asks. "That's awesome. I am so proud of you! When is it?"

"Thanks, it is the day of my nineteenth birthday, April 27th. Isn't that kind of cool?" I grin from ear to ear.

"Wow, you will never forget that for sure. Let me put that on the calendar and let your dad and grandma know so they can come support as well. How did this happen?" She asks while typing fiercely on her phone.

"Remember when I did that poetry tryout for Nike?" I pause and wait until she gives me a head nod yes, "Well the same Nike contact is also working with the people of TEDx Portland and planning the event. I think that's how they got my information and yeah, now I'm going to perform a poem!"

"Wow, you never know who is mentioning your name behind closed doors. That's crazy. You are so amazing. Well get to writing and practicing. I know you will do great." She smiles at me and gives me a hug before returning to her work.

A week later, I still hadn't written anything down. I was stuck! What was I supposed to say in a three-to- four-minute time slot in front of hundreds of people?

I reflect on all the issues I have ever written about and don't know which to focus on. What should my call to action be?

One night when I was struggling at school because of the lack of diversity and the naive shelter culture, I feel like I'm suffocating. I lay in my bed and want to cry. I want God to make everything right, but at the same time, I feel overwhelmed because I don't know where I should start, and then it hits me. I grab a pencil and immediately start writing the poem, "What If?"

I performed on my nineteenth birthday. Backstage I was shaking uncontrollably and mumbling to myself. Some of the staff working the event shot me concerned looks and asked the MC if I would be okay. Everyone was kind and checked in on me, but that didn't do much to calm my nerves. I had never performed in front of such a large audience before. I was still shaking and trembling when I finally grabbed the mic and stepped onto the stage. The first few lines were just as I had rehearsed them, and it wasn't long before I lost myself in the words, stopped trembling and let the faces in the audience fade away from my consciousness.

It was the most thrilling experience ever, and when it was done, I wanted to recite another poem. Everyone praised me and my performance, but what made it all worthwhile was when the event ended, as I was leaving, a stranger stopped me. He was a middle-aged man wearing blue jeans and a button-up shirt. He stood at about five foot nine and had a warm air about him.

"I was watching you live, and I immediately had to come here after hearing your words. That was amazing; thank you for your words and passion." He smiled.

"Thank you so much." I smiled so hard my cheeks hurt.

It may not seem like much, but it is the most fulfilling experience to know another human felt deeply affected by something I did. Sometimes we are quick to limit ourselves or others but if we continue to ask "what if?" we will always exceed our expectations. Asking what-if can achieve change and even make it possible to offer a limitless love to all.

CHANGE

WHAT IF

What if I had three minutes to change the world?
Now before you start to think
I'm just another crazy girl with her silly dreams,
please don't close your eyes and ears,
listen to me.
Because I only have three minutes to change the world,
possibly four,
and I know you're probably thinking,
what can I do in three minutes that you haven't done
   in the years before?

Well, you see we tend to put what, if, and
change in the same sentence,
almost as if it were a dream,
and that's what it seems,
like it's a possibility that's too far to reach.

And then we start saying things like,
we've tried everything to achieve change,
putting people's pain and suffering on TV,
and then we lie back wondering
why people still ignore hunger and poverty.

And notice I didn't say we lie back in our big offices
or we lie back in our beautiful homes
surrounded by family and the comfort of heat.

I didn't say these things because we don't need a
    complex solution.
You don't take a kid suffering from starvation and say
here eat this forty-pound steak!
All he is going to do
is what the world has done to us every time
we offer change to a complex solution,
throw it up in our face.

Harsh,
I know.
But we've pushed change too far
as we continue to watch pain
tear apart homes and families,
always thinking,
but never saying,
change is just too far to reach.

Yet there is something in us...
that thirst,
that hungers after it.
So we continue the pursuit,
the pursuit of something different.
The pursuit of happiness.
The pursuit of change.
But it's like running a race
and in the beginning thinking you are going to lose,
the outcome,
definite defeat.

CHANGE

So we have to change the equation now,
from what if?
To change,
and make it a reality.
So, how, are you wondering,
am I supposed to change the world in
three minutes, possibly four?

I took the equation of change,
and I changed it!
Yes, I was the girl who said
what if my body was like that on TV?
Yes, I was the girl who said what if everyone could just
   like me?
What if my hair were longer?
My skin lighter?
My feet smaller?
My voice higher?

What if I was the definition of beauty
like all those models on TV?
I continued to say what if? about myself
until I realized I am not ugly,
but society,
is.

I went into my closet
reached past the stilettos
grabbed my dirty sneakers,

looked into the mirror with my nappy hair
and said
I
am
beautiful.

I walked out the door and made it a reality.
And if you still don't understand
what I am trying to say,
how about I present it to you another way?

You see, what if time wasn't of the essence?
And enforcing change wasn't my message?
And poetry, not my method
for infiltrating, and motivating people's minds?

You would be amazed at what you'd find
when I spit these words.
Excuse me,
I mean,
when I pronounce these adjectives, verbs and adverbs.

You see, all I want to do is change the world.
If I can have a simple conversation with you
that will give you the motivation to keep trying,
well baby that's when we start living a little more
than dying.
I mean surviving.
I mean all we have to do is listen to our youth.
They're our future,
so watch them work.

CHANGE

As I peel back the cover on their true words
What if?
What if mom and dad weren't gone no more?
What if?
What if stereotypes didn't hit the top but stayed on
   the floor?
What if?
What if education was free?
And I don't mean given to me.

What if
someone believed I could have a dream?
A what if? speech,
And that one day I'd being speaking poetry.
That one day I would be able to scream at the top of
   my lungs
and no-one would assume I am angry.
That one day I would look into the mirror and say 'yes
   that's me.'
Ignorance is bliss is not the key.

What if I had three minutes to change the world?
I would stand in front of thousands of people
and tell them not to change the world but
   themselves, and
common sense, yes!
No!
'cause I learned a long time ago that common sense
isn't common at all.
But the message would still go through,

and they would know what I stand for is true,
and in three minutes,
no, four,
I would have changed the world.

Like a fairy tale,
almost a myth.
I guess it's just what if?
But, what if?

We Ourselves

We ourselves must be rooted in love to make a difference amidst the chaos of this world, but knowing this is not enough. We need to take action. That action should focus on us first so we can be fully equipped to create change.

When CDs were still a thing, I found a Michael Jackson one around my house and put it in the yellow Walkman my grandma had given me for my birthday. The first song was "Man in the Mirror." I remember falling in love with the rhythm and Michael's voice. I was in elementary school at the time, so I don't think I completely understood the lyrics, but the song itself stuck with me through middle school and then high school. In time, the song's message became clear; change is simple; just start with the man or woman in the mirror.

It seems as if almost every time I log on to social media, I find out about a cop or an unarmed Black man who has been killed, or I see hate messages going around. It's easy to get lost in all of the negativity, and to feel overwhelmed. *Is anything going to change? What can I even do? It's just too much!* I wrestle with these thoughts while scrolling through Instagram and Facebook. Sometimes I want to disconnect and look away, but I can't stay away for too long because I also need to be informed. I can't turn away from the fight for justice for all, especially when these conflicts directly impact race relations in America. With everything we are facing in our society today, simply growing up is proving to be a challenge. If I had to bottom-line it, I would say growing up Black in America isn't easy.

What do you do when someone who looks just like you believes that because of how you look, your existence is not that valuable? Or that the pain you have experienced isn't real? Or if they genuinely don't believe a change needs to happen, even in the face of constant injustice? Or what do you do when are told you should just pull yourself up by your bootstraps, but you have never had bootstraps or boots in the first place.

The answer for most of us is, do nothing; because growing up Black in America means encountering other Black people who have been taught we fit a certain stereotype. However, this is not the real problem. The real problem is ignorance and complacency. Those growing up Black in America cannot afford to be ignorant or complacent, and too often, when voices ring out, they are in protest, screams and chants pushing past exhaustion to be heard. How long can these efforts continue? And to what end? Many are left wondering, What's the point? Is it worth it anymore? And What can someone like me do?

Whether we are Black, Brown, yellow, or orange, we can all make a change. We can make a massive difference if we first begin with ourselves. Imagine everyone changing themselves for the better, educating themselves, taking care of themselves, learning, sharing, praying, and trying to be the best version of themselves. Then, the world would indeed be a better place.

Growing up in America means realizing you may not be able to save the world in one night from hatred, but you can make a powerful contribution if you focus on one issue at a time, one day at a time. Start with the person you see in the mirror, and one day, you won't believe how amazing that person is. The world can undergo drastic change as a result of unconditional love. If this form of love were more widely practiced, there would be an inevitable ripple effect that would spread like wildfire. Change in the world can happen one step, one heart, and one relationship at a time. Learning to take the first step in loving ourselves, and understanding how others need to be loved, without condition will help make this world a better place.

Discussion Questions

1. Is the change you desire rooted in love?

2. What does change look like for yourself? For your home environment? For your family? In your community? In your country? In the world?

3. How do you make change happen?

4. What are some struggles you've had when dealing with change?

5. What motivates you to continue to pursue change, and if you don't seek change, why?

CONCLUSION

M y experiences have proven to me how loving unconditionally is necessary for us to live a fruitful and prosperous life. Although it may seem difficult to incorporate unconditional love in our daily lives, doing so makes our lives easier in the long run.

When we learn from God's love for us and love ourselves unconditionally, we are setting up all of our relationships for success. In loving ourselves, we are taking care of ourselves. Therefore, by not expecting anyone else to do that for us, others can love us for who we are instead of trying to save us. More importantly, others get to love a healthy version of us, which is the best version to love. So again, if we are to be loved by anyone in this world, it should be first by ourselves.

Within our marriages and families, we learn we can maintain a healthy balance of interaction with loved ones through unconditional love because we won't focus on everything they don't do for us. Instead, we now focus on what is best for them, which gives them space to grow and be loved by us and keeps us from unnecessary conflict or nagging.

Unconditional love is a reminder that when our kids may seem ungrateful, or *are* ungrateful, their life is a gift in itself, and there is no repayment they can give to us that would ever measure up to how we feel about them. It is a reminder to step back and breathe and continue to teach while understanding they are still learning how to love. After all, we are the example.

Unconditional love is at the heart of helping others and making a difference. If we don't seek to change the world out of love for its inhabitants, how can we contribute to making it better and not worse? I continue to pray and wrestle with not forcing others to be like me and to allow them the space to grow at their own pace. Still, when they blossom, it is mind-blowing and leaves no question that loving unconditionally is the best way forward.

I know it's crazy to think about loving the mailman who drops off your mail, or the random couple walking their dog, or the kids playing in the park when you do not know who they are. Yet it's worth being uncomfortable. When we love unconditionally, we open an ample number of opportunities for not just the people we know, but also for those we don't. This way they, too, can be happy, learn, and grow into more loving human beings. Although it may not happen overnight, this is something we are all inevitably striving for, a better and more loving world to exist and raise our families safely in. If I've learned anything from my life, it's that no matter what I do or think I want, I need unconditional love. My family needs unconditional love. The world needs unconditional love, and it is through God that we can craft our model.

Now that you know how unconditional love can make a positive impact on our daily lives and how much we need it, it's time to take some steps to begin your own journey. The action that follows is what helps us grow. There are three essential and final steps to help propel us forward to becoming the individuals we desire to become.

Step 1

Before we do anything, we need to first have a relationship with God and understand that, not only does he love us unconditionally, but there is absolutely nothing we can do to change that. The best part about this is that even if we don't have an existing relationship with God, he still loves us and is waiting for us to create that relationship; a relationship you can start by praying, picking up a bible or going to your local church. If you have an existing relationship with God, but maybe you don't talk with him as much as you would like, he is still waiting for you and doesn't love you less because of this. Pursue God, and you will receive his unconditional love. It is through his unconditional love that you will learn you are enough and so deserving of only the best.

Step 2

Love yourself as God loves you. You are perfectly and wonderfully made, and you should never doubt that. We are human beings, and we live in a society that constantly reinforces why we should doubt our worth and beauty, but know that you need no condition to be loved because your existence is amazing. There is no other you, and there will never be. That is already great, but now add the fact that God the Almighty, Alpha, and Omega loves you just as you are. That makes it even better. Take care of yourself physically, mentally, and spiritually by showing yourself love, because you deserve the best, and it begins with you.

Step 3

Practice loving others unconditionally. Start with family first and strengthen all of your relationships by learning to get rid of conditions while maintaining healthy boundaries. If you can set healthy boundaries with family members, setting them with strangers will be even easier. You can choose one relationship at a time to work on and provide the support that is rooted in a condition-less environment so they know you truly love them and only want the best. Then, as you become more comfortable, you can work your way up to the relationship that needs more work. Regardless of the step you are on, the point is to start loving unconditionally now and to transform not only your life, but also others you care about.

We wrestled with unconditional love in relation to family, acceptance, happiness, love, racism, spirituality, and more throughout this book. The intention is to help shape and continue to chisel away at identity to form the best version of ourselves. Are we perfect now? Maybe not, but we have started on an important journey. We can't turn back now.

We've had difficult conversations or plan on having those conversations in the future, and make new decisions, and focus on growth, so don't stop pushing forward. Just because the book is over doesn't mean your desire and search for the truth and how to love unconditionally has to stop. I pray my book has planted a seed in you or someone you love to continue this journey. Continue to ask difficult questions, invest in your relationships, and know you are a beautiful human being.

I would love to know some of your conversations or the discoveries you've made while reading this book. If you are interested in sharing some of your journey with me, please visit my website at asiagreene.org or connect with me on Instagram at @asiagreene.

ACKNOWLEDGEMENTS

To the love of my life, Demetrius Kalen Rhodes, who has pushed me every day to write this book and to do what makes me happy; thank you for pushing me to finish. Thank you for encouraging me when I wanted to throw in the towel and reminding me that I don't suck. I love you.

To my mom and dad who have always believed in me and in my writing ever since I was a child. I am truly grateful for all you do. From amazing advice, giving me room to safely make mistakes and grow from them, to pursuing my dreams, thank you. I am so happy you have both been in my corner cheering me on to take this big step.

To my grandma who is definitely my number one fan, I can't wait for you to read this so you can say your granddaughter finally published a book. I love you Grandma!

To my siblings, thank you for all the support, real feedback, encouragement, and love.

To Ashley Ormon, for your patience in every lesson you reminded me of or taught me. Thank you for being honest and real with me.

ABOUT THE AUTHOR

ASIA GREENE-RHODES

A sia Greene has always held a passion for personal growth and making a difference. After receiving a master's degree in Education from George Fox University, she continued to foster her love for spoken word poetry. Her insightful and provoking words led her to presenting on numerous stages, including at TEDx and Nike events. After becoming an educator and starting a lifestyle blog, she began writing her debut book from her collection of poems. She was born and raised in Portland, Oregon. When she isn't writing—or performing spoken word, she can be found sipping Earl Grey tea, spending time with her family and friends, or working out.

Connect with Asia

asiagreene.org
Instagram @asiagreene
Facebook facebook.com/asia.greene.98

CPSIA information can be obtained
at www.ICGtesting.com
Printed in the USA
LVHW110016230422
716845LV00009BA/403